PERFECTION
OF THE
MORNING

PERFECTION OF THE MORNING

A Woman's Awakening in Nature

SHARON BUTALA

Hungry Mind Press
Saint Paul, Minnesota

To Those Who Knew This Land in Ancient Times

Published by Hungry Mind Press
98 Snelling Avenue North
Saint Paul, Minnesota 55104

Published by arrangement with HarperSanFrancisco, a division of
HarperCollins Publishers, Inc.

Originally published in Canada as *The Perfection of the Morning: An
Apprenticeship in Nature*: first in hardcover in 1994 by HarperCollins
Publishers Ltd, Toronto, Canada; then as a HarperPerennial paper-
back in 1995.

9 8 7 6 5 4 3 2 1
First Hungry Mind Press Printing, 1997

Library of Congress Catalog Card Number: 96-78758

Printed in the United States of America

CONTENTS

PREFACE

In 1976 when I was thirty-six years old I married my second husband, Peter, and came here to live on his ranch in the extreme southwest corner of Saskatchewan, just north of the Montana border. Although I'd been born in Saskatchewan and had lived here all but five years of my life, I had arrived in a landscape that, although I found it extraordinary, was not only unfamiliar to me, but of a kind I hadn't even known existed in this province. I hadn't studied it in school, since no early explorer had crossed it, no one going this far south, the miles and miles of open plains being as daunting as an ocean to a nineteenth-century traveler. In my car trips across the country I hadn't seen it, since no major highways went through its heart; everyone I knew holidayed either in the lake country of the north, or the Qu'Appelle Valley in the southeast, while southwest Saskatchewan, as far as I knew, had only the tiny man-made lake in the center of Cypress Hills Park, and no major river systems. Now it seems amazing that I knew nothing about a place that covers about 28,000 square kilometers, is five times the size of Prince Edward Island and slightly bigger than Vermont.

Southwest Saskatchewan is best grasped as part of the vast Great Plains of North America which extend north to Edmonton and south into Texas. It's a high plateau—the Butala ranch is at a typical one thousand meters—and it seemed from the first time Peter took me there that I knew this, as the terrain and even the air in some nebulous way seem to breathe of altitude. Its topography is low rolling hills and flat or sloping grassy areas cut here and there by coulees, chasms of varying sizes eroded by rain and meltwater in which shrubs or, in the larger ones, trees, often coniferous, grow. There are virtually no trees growing naturally elsewhere — a nearby municipality is called Lonetree — and no other shelter. Coulees provide the only refuge from the insistent, inescapable burn of the summer sun or from winter blizzards, and are havens for deer, rabbits and other small animals and birds. They are always fascinating places to explore since their steep clay sides provide dens for bobcats or coyote families and high places for golden eagles to anchor their large, reusable nests built of sticks.

The climate is one of extremes, with temperatures ranging from minus fifty Celsius to highs of plus forty Celsius. A constant, steady wind in winter brings on blizzards of appalling severity and in the summer heat, tornadoes which, because of the thin and scattered population, usually do little damage, and are frequently not even reported. The severe climate I was used to as a native Saskatchewanian, but, also used to battling mountains of snow all winter, I was surprised to find that some winters, month after month, the pale ground, frozen hard as rock, would be covered by only the occasional skiff of thin, dry snow. In the early years, before I'd gotten used to the winters here, I found it depressing to look out my kitchen window and see, instead of fields of glistening snow shading from purple to blue to white to silver, dun-colored barrenness day after day all the long winter. But this area of the province is blessed with Chinooks, too, which blow in from Alberta now and then during the winter, their warm winds taking away what snow there is, and bringing sudden, spring-like temperatures in the midst of the deepest cold.

As the American writer Wallace Stegner — a resident of Eastend (the town nearest us) from 1914 to 1920 — has pointed out, the true West on both sides of the border is defined by its aridity, and in practical terms, settlement has always been determined by the availability of drinkable water, of a reliable supply for livestock, and sufficient moisture to grow crops. I didn't know it at the time, but the place I was about to call home is situated in the driest part of a region so dry the annual precipitation runs to only about thirty-one centimeters (twelve inches).

Water is indeed a scarce resource: the lack of it determines also the flora — species which conserve water, like cactus — the fauna — which must be able to go long distances for water, or to make do with little of it — and the livelihood of its inhabitants. After I'd been here for a while I began to sense that the constant worry about having enough of it for even the most basic needs also helps set the character of the people, for the older generation tends to be determined sometimes to the point of rigidity, having a touch of grimness which makes belly laughs fewer than rare, who instead find relief in a more reliable laconic, dry humor.

As in much of the true West, rivers are few, small and tend to run dry in drought years. South of the South Saskatchewan, the region's northern boundary, the only true river is the Frenchman, which runs out of the Cypress Hills, more or less southeasterly till it crosses the border into Montana near Val Marie, eventually emptying into the Missouri-Mississippi river system. The Frenchman was once called the "White Mud," after the outcroppings of high-quality white clay that gleam in the sun on bare cliffs along the river valleys. To this day that clay is mined in the Ravenscrag valley running west of Eastend, and carted off daily to Medicine Hat where it is turned into irrigation tiles and sundry other ceramic utensils and vessels.

Before the advent of settlers or even ranchers, the river was called the Frenchman in the United States and the White Mud in Canada, and on early maps (I have seen one dated 1875), there was a gap between the two. When it was demonstrated that they were the same river — how can I help but wonder who first made that trip of discovery, although his name is unrecorded?—the name was changed in Canada to the Frenchman. The other major streams are both called creeks: Swift Current Creek and the historic Battle Creek — "historic" because the Cypress Hills Massacre took place there in the spring of 1873, the event which finally brought the North-West Mounted Police to the West. During the worst drought years all three creeks may run dry, at least in places where there are no springs feeding them.

The area, in fact, had been designated historically as too dry for farming. It is part of the Palliser Triangle, a term not quite synonymous with southwest Saskatchewan, since the Triangle runs into southeastern Alberta. The area acquired this name through Captain John Palliser, an Irish army officer sent out by the British under the auspices of the Royal Geographical Society in 1857 to survey some of the Canadian West as to its suitability for agriculture. His report, not published till 1869, described a triangular area having the American-Canadian border for its base between 100 and 114 degrees longitude, with its apex at 52 degrees latitude, including most, if not all, of southwest Saskatchewan as unsuitable for agriculture.

But the Canadian government soon became eager to prevent Americans, whose policy of Manifest Destiny was causing them to look over the border with a grimly acquisitive eye, from simply riding their horses into this uninhabited area and calling it their own. Palliser's report was a deterrent to settlement for a while but in time, with the encouragement of others who traveled over and studied the same territory, bringing back more favorable reports (none of them, Palliser included, reaching as far south as where I sit writing), it was opened to farming regardless. Palliser's pronouncement, although an unwelcome and frequently maligned one, contains enough truth that it can't be erased, and to this day it hangs over the land.

The most striking geographical feature, and the one even I had heard about, is the Cypress Hills north of here, lying across the Alberta-Saskatchewan border and extending so far south and east as to account for Eastend's name. The hills peak at an extraordinary 1,392 meters, the highest point in Canada between the Rocky Mountains and a high point in Labrador. There are no cypresses in the Cypress Hills: the lodgepole pines which actually grow there were misnamed by the Métis, who used the word to mean "jack pine." Because of their straightness and height, these pines were used by the Natives as tepee poles.

Not only are the Hills beautiful but, together with a tip in the Wood Mountains about three hundred kilometers southeast, they are unique in the West. During the Pleistocene ten to twelve million years ago when glaciers scraped down this area, the highest part of the Hills remained above the level of the ice. To this day certain montane species of flora, which occur elsewhere only in the Rocky Mountains two hundred miles to the west, can be found there.

The climate and fauna of the Hills are different enough from the rolling grasslands that surround them; locally they are considered to be the showplace of the area. But familiar as I was with forest, the wooded Cypress Hills didn't hold nearly the appeal for me that the great sweeps of short-grass prairie south of them did. Standing in a field of six-inch to foot-high grass, or driving down a road with the long fields opening out to each side of me ending in a low line of blue hills at the bottom of the sky, I felt I had at last been freed into the elements. It was as if places where I'd lived, the forests of my birthplace in the north, those of Nova Scotia, and the mountains and ocean of lower mainland British Columbia, were all merely mistakes of Nature. It seemed to me that I had at last found the one true landscape, the place where sun, moon and stars could shine free, lending their light to the pale grasses, painting them gleaming apricot, gold, mauve, or rose. I had never seen such beauty.

I didn't have the slightest inkling of it that weekend almost eighteen years ago when I first saw this place, but I had arrived here at a turning point in its history. The last equally momentous turning point had occurred in the 1870s when the hundreds of thousands of buffalo that wandered here were hunted to virtual extinction. The loss of the base of the Native culture, especially of its principal food source, was in part responsible for the Cree and Plains Ojibwa finally agreeing in 1874 to sign Treaty Number Four, and the Blackfoot to sign Treaty Number Seven in 1877. Then the original, nomadic way of life led by the Plains' people for thousands of years came to a tragic end, and a new one, that of agriculture by Europeans, began.

The treaties removed Native people from the area, making it safe for ranchers, often American, to use it as grazing land for their great herds of cattle. Southwest Saskatchewan quickly became the home of famous, huge ranches: the Z–X (read as "zed bar x" or "zee bar ex" as its American owners would have pronounced it), the Turkey Track, the Matador, the Wallace and Ross spread, actually an Alberta ranch so enormous its leased land ran into Saskatchewan, and the T–Down — on part of which Peter and I now live and have our hay farm.

Gradually over the next twenty years the ranchers were forced to give way little by little to farmers. Today most of the vast stretches of short-grass have been plowed up to grow crops, mostly durum and spring wheats, forever changing the appearance of the landscape, and of course providing the death knell, although other forces have been at work, too, for most of the ranches.

When I arrived here, the second period of major change was already poised to begin. Soon conditions came together — sufficient rain, a rise in wheat prices, benevolent government policies — which resulted in a sudden prosperity such as southwest Saskatchewan had never known, and which people saw as the fulfillment at last of the hopeful prophecies of those who lured settlers into this inhospitable country seventy-five years before. Nobody then had any idea that the bonanza would be only an ironic footnote to a much greater and more sorrowful, if still incomplete, metamorphosis. If during my first years here I often bitterly regretted my decision to come here to live, looking back, I would not now choose otherwise, not the least of the reasons being because of the privilege, however appalling at times, of being witness to the second tragic transformation.

Having made the fateful decision to throw up my former life in favor of a brand-new one, if in the beginning I often found myself having a difficult, even painful time in finding a social footing and in feeling I could ever be a member of my new society of rural, agricultural people, in my awe at the beauty and openness of the landscape, I felt as if my soul had at last found its home. Slowly, through my joy in the beauty of this new landscape, I began to learn new things, to see my life differently. I began to realize how life for all of us in the West is informed and shaped by Nature in ways we don't even realize, much less notice consciously. Eventually, all that I was learning led to this book.

The other day a woman friend remarked how she struggled to make her life "congruent." I hadn't heard that term before, and psychobabble or not, it struck me as apt. It seems to me an accurate description of how I feel my life is now in the important ways. I came a stranger to this magnificent but in some ways terrible place to live, with its more tragic than triumphant history, and gradually, although never easily, I found both a way to feel at home in my own skin, and in this place.

Through that struggle to fit — to become congruent — I became not the painter I once was but a writer, and I discovered that the writer I've become is the Self I've been in search of for so many years. But at the same time it has been the act of writing that created and continues to create that Self I've at last found, and that acts as the instrument of integration between myself and my environment, chiefly my home in the landscape. The last seventeen years here have been a long, intensely personal spiritual journey, one that has been inextricably intertwined with my reacquaintance with the land and the effects of this renewed relationship with Nature on my own woman's soul.

The Perfection of the Morning began as a small, impersonal book about building a relationship with Nature. As I wrote and rewrote, I began to see that there was no separating my spiritual journey, my life, from the reasons for and the effects of my daily contact with Nature. Although I did not want to write autobiography and for a long time avoided it as much as I could, the book kept growing, and I gradually recognized that it would have to become autobiography, at least to the extent that would make clear my themes.

But nonetheless, there's a way in which all nonfiction is fiction: the backward search through happenstance, trivia, the flotsam and jetsam of life to search out a pattern, themes, a meaning is by its nature an imposition of order onto what was chaotic. It's an attempt to give a linearity to events, many psychic, which had no linearity, which, if anything, were a spiral, or had more the hectic quality of a dream. What is true are thoughts, dreams, visions. What may or may not be true are the order and timing of events, the perception and linking of them. If it's true on the one hand that everything is what it seems to be, and I constantly remind myself of this, on the other, there is a way in which it's also true that nothing is. I begin to think like the Bushmen, as Laurens van der Post reports them as believing, that in the beginning a dream was dreaming us, and like Clifton Fadiman who said that the older he gets the more his life seems to him to have been, rather than a series of actual events, one long, interesting dream. In writing what the world will call autobiography, I am torn between the facts and history and the truth of the imagination, and it is to the latter, finally, in terms of my personal history, that I lean.

In terms of the people and the land — their history, the economics of the area, the statistics, and the current situation — I have tried to be as accurate factually as possible.

DREAM COYOTE

The day I left Saskatoon for good, I had sold my house, abandoned a promising job teaching at the university as well as my nearly completed master's degree, and said farewell to a circle of good women friends and to my mother and three of my four sisters and their families who lived there. I was both rather proud of my own daring and a little appalled at it; the image of a burning bridge was strong in my mind, and I stoked the flames gleefully, with a feeling close to triumph.

Although they said nothing, I knew both my friends and my family thought I was making a terrible mistake. Such is the prestige of a university job, the sense of those who make a life there as being the anointed, that my fellow graduate students and lecturers must have found my abdication from it very hard to understand. If my mother and sisters were collectively holding their breaths, not wanting to pass judgment and hoping against hope for the best, I knew my friends expected me to be back, newly divorced, in a year if not sooner, for marriage breakdown was happening all around us at the time — divorce, separation, reshuffling of couples, more split-ups, more divorces, more unhappiness.

And the truth was, in that first two or three years of my new life, I often said to myself that if I'd really understood what I was getting into, I'd never have done it, not realizing before I left that if my own family and friends had their private doubts about our marriage, the same was true of Peter's family, his friends, even his hired man. In my new life I would have to learn to deal with, at the least, skeptical glances, and for every person who was welcoming, there would be no shortage of people who, though they ought to have been at least silent, if not kind, on the subject of my suitability as a wife for Peter were neither.

Peter had been born and had never lived anywhere else but on the remote family ranch in the Old Man On His Back range of hills, south of the Cypress Hills, and north of the peaked, purple line of the Bears Paw Mountains in Montana. Unlike most of the city men I knew, he didn't nourish in secret bitterness unfulfilled dreams about another, better life; he loved his life as a cowboy-rancher and rural man. And, too, he was secure in his community, surrounded by men he'd gone to school with, cowboyed with, had good times with as far back as he could remember, who'd married and whose wives he'd known since childhood, and whose children were being raised into the same rural, agricultural world as their parents and grandparents and sometimes even great-grandparents had been.

Maybe it was his calmness, engendered by the deep sense of security stemming from a life lived all in one place, and of his sense of the rightness of his life that attracted me. But looking back, I see such a complicated mix of factors: the man, yes, but also the greenness and beauty of the landscape, and the smell of the air, the cool, sharp wind that swept away those things that in my city life I had thought were inevitable and unavoidable.

I first visited this place eighteen years ago on a twenty-fourth of May weekend when I drove down with my son, Sean. Peter had invited us months before, but I hadn't wanted to come, thinking that a ranch held no attractions for me. Peter repeated the invitation and Sean, all boy, had been begging me to go, till I finally gave in. Through a mix-up about dates (the twenty-fourth of May weekend didn't fall on the twenty-fourth that year), the day we arrived at the hay farm Peter was taken aback to see us. He and some other men were hard at work rounding up his cattle, sorting them, and loading them into huge trucks (called cattle liners) to haul them south to the ranch for the summer, since for a variety of reasons, including uncooperative weather, it was too late in the year to trail them on horseback the forty miles as he usually did. He explained to us that the cattle spend most of the year on the ranch, but winters they're trailed to the hay farm in the Frenchman River valley where the supply of winter feed is grown. This is a more economical alternative to moving the feed to the cattle. Peter was embarrassed because he couldn't leave his work to act the proper host and had to leave us pretty much to fend for ourselves.

I spent the entire day perched on the corral watching the men work. There is a snapshot of me sitting there, my hair well down below my shoulders, wearing jeans and a thick siwash-like sweater, which always reminds me of B.B. King since I bought it the same day I heard him perform at the Montreal Forum, in what was one of the highlights of my life (overshadowed only by the time in 1965 when I'd heard a young Bob Dylan perform in a half-empty Queen Elizabeth Theatre in Vancouver).

I was so fascinated by what I saw that the day flew by, even though all I did was sit and watch. Sean sat with me at first, but then he helped in the chute loading cattle into the trucks, and was nearly trampled by a steer when it backed down the chute, turned around, and was about to run over anybody who got in his way.

"Climb the corral! Climb the corral!" the men shouted at him, as Sean and the thousand-pound steer faced off and I watched, too dumb even to realize his life was, quite seriously, in danger, since the steer might avoid him, but more likely wouldn't. Sean, twelve at the time, leaped to the side of the chute and scrambled up the corral rail with the agility that marked him as a young athlete, so that my heart swelled with pride. Later there was a branding, and Peter invited Sean to help wrestle calves, an invitation Sean eagerly accepted. When Peter teasingly invited me to do the same, I laughed and said no thanks.

I think now that if there hadn't been that confusion about which weekend we were to arrive, and Peter had taken the days off to do as he usually did for visitors — drive them around the countryside, show them the ranch, saddle horses and take them for a ride — I would have said, Ho hum, gone away and never come back again. But the privilege of actually seeing the real work of the ranch and all the things that went with it had a different effect on me. I remember afterward laughingly telling my mother we'd spent the weekend in the middle of a Roy Rogers movie, but if I joked with her about it, and if Sean viewed it as an entertaining but not-to-be-repeated adventure which he soon forgot about, I was actually stirred so deeply that everything in my old life — friends, job, family, politics — paled beside it.

It wasn't just the scenery or the novelty of everything that captivated me. I was struck also by how comfortable those men had seemed, how at ease they were in their work, and how unassuming and casual in their skill with the animals and with the tools they used to manage them. I was surprised to see they were actually enjoying themselves. They laughed, cracked jokes, kidded each other while they worked in the corral or on horseback, roped, or cut out cattle and chased them in. I was used to a world perpetually fraught with tension, with competitiveness so extreme at times as to seem really crazy, where the only constant was steady but, nonetheless, gut-wrenching change and the resulting mad scrabbling for position. As I sat on the rail watching and listening that day a new world was washing slowly over me, seeping in without my noticing, a slower world, and a timeless one that resonated with a sense that it must always have been there in just this way and always would be.

It had been an unusually wet spring, and although it wasn't warm, the hills and grassy plains were as green and inviting as Ireland, so that my first look at the area was, to this extent, deceptive. As I look back to that weekend such a long time ago, when my world changed forever, the memory is dreamlike: the men riding their horses at a walk through the tall green grass and wildflowers on the riverbank, the wave of sloping green hills behind them, the clarity and the veracity of the light, in the lulls between wind gusts the music of birds, the splash of the shallow brown river running by below the corrals, the click of the cattle's hooves, the cowboy ululations of the men.

I had never lived on a farm. Both my parents had come from farms, though: my mother from southern Manitoba and my father first from a farm near Magog, Quebec, and then from near St. Isidore de Bellevue, Saskatchewan, about seven miles from Batoche, the site of the Riel Rebellion in 1884–5, the trenches of which may still be seen, as well as the bullet holes in the little church. I have sometimes wondered if my father, who didn't speak English himself till he learned it at school in Bellevue, had heard from his French-speaking teachers in that French community about Louis Riel, Gabriel Dumont, and the battle fought just down the road from where they sat. Even though we have no Native blood that I know of, I do remember him mentioning Dumont more than once in a way that suggested the name and possibly the events were a part of his community's folklore. In those days, around 1912, there would not have been Native children in school with him, although many of the children must have been Métis, since Batoche was the heart of the Métis community in the old Northwest. But all that is an aside. It was a farming community and the Le Blancs, too, having come as farmers to Acadia in the mid-seventeenth century, were still farmers.

My sisters and I came from pioneering families on both sides: both sets of grandparents had homesteaded, as had our parents, so that "the homestead" was part of our basic vocabulary, a term we must have learned along with "mother," "father" and "bread." Our Irish-Canadian grandfather, Francis Graham, was even said to have been born under the wagonbox near Portage-la-Prairie, Manitoba, as his family trekked, in the early 1880s, from their home in Ontario to the West. Their original Manitoba farm was established in 1884, a Centennial Farm, a fact of which the family is inordinately, and justifiably, proud. On that side of the family our children are fifth-generation westerners.

This is how it was that my sisters and I grew up with the notion of the farm as a mythic paradise from which we had been expelled, by drought and bankers, and could never return. Basic as it was to us, though, having never lived on a farm much less a ranch, which belonged to some other tradition than our family's, we viewed the notion as city dwellers do, quizzically, with a touch of apprehension, possibly even a little distaste.

In the years since the summer I turned thirteen and we moved to the city, I had become so urbanized that I knew nothing about farming, or about the daily life led by people who made their living in agriculture. I thought of myself proudly as a sophisticated city woman, but even that first weekend with Peter, strangely, I kept having flashes of déjà vu. They were incomplete, vague and unformed, and yet carried with them a puzzling tug of recognition, of memories that were more visceral even than images or fragments of conversations. Bewilderingly, I felt comfortable when I should have felt ill at ease; I felt at home when I should have felt lost. The can of evaporated milk on the table we used for our coffee, the orange offered me for dessert, the denseness of the air, the smell, the feeling of being close to the earth in the log house where we stayed were all *just so* to me; I felt transported to a familiar way of being and to a familiar place. Yes, I thought, and then, but how do I know this?

Gradually, over the year of our courtship, I began to remember what I had deliberately forgotten, how I had spent the first four years of my life in wilderness, living in log or hastily thrown together frame shacks in what we call the bush in northern Saskatchewan. I was conceived there, carried for nine months in my mother's body there, knew no other place for those first formative years. My earliest memories are of nuggets of sunlight glinting off shoulder-high, damp emerald grass, of playing in the roots of trees, of the ephemeral, terrifying beauty of the northern lights, of the soul-stirring wail of timber wolves, of our mother setting coal oil lamps in windows to keep bears away, of mountains of snow and impassable, muddy or "corduroy" roads, boggy stretches which settlers covered with unpeeled slabs of trees for wagons or cars to bump over, and the richness of the texture, scent, the vibrant *color* of the air of northern Saskatchewan.

For a time my mother's parents rented a farm somewhere north of Prince Albert or Nipawin: the feel of the hot sandy road on our bare feet as Cynthia, my older sister, and I whiled away the interminable summer afternoons while our grandparents napped, having been up since dawn, playing in our grandmother's garden where with our cousins we built bowers and planted cities and made celebratory avenues out of plucked pinks, pansies, bachelor's buttons and daisies, waiting for our mothers to come and collect us. And the violent northern storms where we sat indoors with our feet up off the floor as lightning cracked and thunder boomed all around the small log house, the swaying yellow lanterns, the feathery legs of our grandfather's big work horses, their huge feet and their quiet steady air, our grandmother smiling and silent, as if meditating, as she sat moving the paddle of the butter churn up and down for hours in the kitchen, morning after morning spooning up the breakfast porridge from her blue willow bowls till the sad lovers and the weeping willow between them were revealed again.

In that setting at the hay farm, the color and feel of an orange in my hand, the can of milk on the table were suddenly freighted with meaning beyond the immediate circumstances, meaning that at first I could not quite decipher. I was now beginning to remember the early childhood I had chosen to forget as both valueless and unsuitable for the person I had been trying to become. As I remembered it, I began slowly to reclaim it in surprise and delight, for in this new context it was valued, something to be proud of, a treasury of meaning, facts, knowledge. I didn't consciously think so at the time, but in some ways it began to seem that instead of coming to a new place, I had come home.

As time passed and I visited the hay farm occasionally, the rural setting with the Frenchman River running past the house, I remembered too the Saskatchewan River from a later time in my childhood when we'd lived in a village on its banks before the damming of it. I remembered the crash and roar of the ice going out in the spring, especially the spring it almost took the great black iron bridge with it, and our father (with the

Mounties' permission) bravely walking out onto it, just to feel the power of the river, I guess, as we waited, breathless and awestruck, on the bank for him either to be swept away forever or to return to us. The river's great, wild presence came back to me, its spirit which hovered over it and around it and in it and which affected everyone who came near it touched me again; I could even recall its heavy, scented odor.

What I could remember about that natural world from which our family had been separated by so little was a combination of smells, the feel of the air, a sense of the presence of Nature as a living entity all around me. All of that had been deeply imprinted in me, but more in the blood and bone and muscles — an instinctive memory — than a precise memory of events or people. I remembered it with my body, or maybe I remembered it with another sense for which we have no name but is no less real for that. As I returned to the ranch and hay farm to visit, the sense of this memory grew; I found myself inexorably drawn to it although I did not understand this at the time, preferring to accept the obvious romantic scenario of marrying and living happily ever after.

If I could recover my powerful early connections with Nature, there was still the reality that as I became a town and then a city child, I had stopped thinking of Nature as people raised in it do and began to think of it as urban people do: as a place to holiday — the mountains, the seaside, a quiet lake somewhere in the country — as a place to acquire a suntan, have a summer romance, paint a picture of, enjoy a change of atmosphere. For a long period in my late teens and early twenties, I actively avoided picnics, complaining bitterly that they were stupid since there were always dirt and bugs and leaves in your food and insects to bite you, and although they were supposed to be a holiday, picnics were more work for us women than cooking a meal in the kitchen would be.

Besides, though born in the bush into relative poverty I had, for whatever reasons, learned to aspire to a more glamorous lifestyle — at six, never having seen a dancer other than my father stepdancing late at night at a farmhouse party somewhere, I wanted to be a ballet dancer; I wanted to wear satin ballgowns, go to the theater, have movie stars for friends. I did not want to go back to the bush, a place so terrible that my mother, once we were gone from there, wouldn't even speak of it. When I asked about it when she was an old woman, she told me that she tried never to think of it, and on her deathbed, when I asked again, her response came in a distant whisper, her eyes dark and fixed on something I couldn't see: "It was so cold . . . the wind was always blowing . . . in the morning . . . the men would . . . put on their things and go out . . ." She fell into silence and I regretted asking her, and yet I wanted to know, I truly wanted to know.

There was indeed a whole other story, a narrative, our family history transformed into our family mythology, which was what I had grown into since the other — the compelling, intense beauty of Nature and our lives lived in the midst of it — was never spoken of, never even conceived of in any concrete way in all the years since we'd left. Our father said nothing; our mother painted golden pictures of her girlhood on the prosperous farm in Manitoba, which I at least doubted, although I never dared say so. (And a good thing, too, because long after her death, when I paid my only visit there, I saw that they had all been true.) We had come from better things — land ownership and wealth, ancient heroism, blood links to the aristocracy in Ireland and Scotland — our fortunes had fallen, but we as people had not fallen with them, and consequently we did not dwell on the hardships, the misfortunes, the demeaning struggles for survival, refusing to accept them as anything more than temporary conditions to be met with courage and disdain.

I think, in accepting about our family history what I was told, I was often confused by the contrast between it and the life I had lived. I couldn't doubt what my mother said, yet these ancient family memories were no more to me than fairy tales. (As I grew older, in fact, I persisted in identifying with my father's family.) I was too young at the time to have been able to keep clear mental pictures of my own of our life in the bush into which I was born, but from my own diffuse memories in combination with our few ragged black-and-white snapshots, and eventually our mother's mother's memoirs, the images I knew were not inviting. The family stories, not often mentioned, were about hardship: people hurt or ill or losing or having babies, doctors miles away over bad or impassable roads and stories about survival in the cold; about the hard, hard labor of the men to provide the most meager kind of existence for us under conditions that were often heartbreaking, the most instructive of these being how, according to our grandmother's memoirs, during the Depression when our families ran out of cash, our father and our mother's father would spend an entire day in the bush cutting a couple of cords of firewood which they would take to town and sell for one dollar and fifty cents a cord. And once our grandfather had to carry one hundred pounds of flour on his back a mile and a half through the water and bog that had swallowed the road into his and our grandmother's log house.

But there also had been much laughter. Our mother and our aunts sometimes talked, when we were young, about the funny things that had happened, the practical jokes, the visiting with neighbors; there was even much laughter about the hardship, trailing off into muted smiles and finally silence freighted with a painful and, it seemed to me, confused nostalgia.

Even though that past which had become somehow shameful was hardly ever mentioned — such a fall it was for our mother and her family — as I grew up this was what I remembered. It had become far more important than the other — the life lived so close to Nature — which also was never spoken of. (Although I remember our mother, in her seventies at the time, saying in a dreamy voice with a faint smile, how our father "used to shoot ptarmigan." "Really? Ptarmigan?" I said. She looked at me, her distant smile vanishing, returned to her small house in Saskatoon where we sat together. "I think it was ptarmigan," she said. "I think it was your father.")

By the time I was twenty I had developed contempt for those who wanted to return to Nature, believing they were all romantic dreamers, nitwits from the city, people raised in the lap of luxury who did not know about Nature's nasty side, who had never done a day's real work in their lives and thus had no idea of the grinding labor a life in Nature demanded for mere survival. I liked to look at Impressionist paintings of Nature, having once harbored the dream of becoming a painter, and I was not averse to sunsets or moonlight on water, but I was just as happy to look at pictures of them while seated on a soft couch, with my feet on a thick rug and a well-insulated wall between me and the thing itself.

Yet driving home from some errand in Regina, late at night on a deserted and lonely highway, I often looked out my side window and saw above the hills a few small white stars, points of light in boundless darkness. Once, as I gazed up at them, my heart, a live thing in my chest, leaped, cracked and then hung there, aching. At that moment it seemed a thing apart from the *me* I knew, and it yearned with an intensity that was deeply sorrowful to go back to the immensity from which it declared itself to have come.

And, driving down for short visits in the year before our marriage, I used to wait for that first moment when I neared the ranch, when the country seemed to open up, and I saw again the wide fields of native grass cured, very quickly even after that wet, green spring, to a pale yellow by the sun, for with that sight came the much longed-for lifting of my heart, a metaphorical unfurrowing of my brow, the easing of my muscles, and the city life, my studies, my urban concerns fell away from me. It was as if in that magnificent spread of pure light across the grassy miles I could breathe freely for the first time since childhood.

Peter and I decided very soon after my first visit here that we would marry, but we both agreed, each for our own reasons, that it would be better to wait till the following spring. The winter was a long one, and at Christmas, leaving behind the round of parties and my long, silky dresses, I drove down with Sean to spend the week with Peter on the ranch.

It was my first lesson in the realities of ranching life. Although none of this made clear sense to me at the time, every winter the Butalas, on horseback, trailed their cattle the forty miles from the ranch northeast to the hay farm where there was shelter in the breaks of the Frenchman

River and a winter's supply of hay and grain bales. Every spring they trailed them back south to spend late spring, summer and fall on the ranch where the great fields of grazing land were. Each move took three days, and sometimes four, since they were willing to travel at a pace comfortable to the cattle.

Peter took it for granted that I would do this without questioning it, and since I had no idea what I was getting into, I naively didn't. I got up one morning and soon found myself, with Sean beside me, driving the half-ton loaded with square bales behind a four-hundred-head herd of twelve-hundred-pound range cows and two- and three-year-old steers and heifers. Between the half-ton and the herd were four men on horseback, and out of sight up ahead, another led the way in the four-wheel-drive ton truck.

I had never seen anybody move cattle before, and I knew nothing about range cattle. Peter's cattle were (and are) horned Herefords, beautiful, powerful animals whose strong white horns can kill with one well-aimed thrust, but I hardly knew enough to be afraid of them. Except in the most vague sense, I did not know where we were going — to a road allowance somewhere where we'd pen them for the night — or even very clearly why. I was in a kind of culture shock, at once bewildered, frightened, excited.

That winter there was an unusually large amount of snow which was in places, even out on the open and windswept plains, very deep. Since we were crossing uninhabited grassland that first day, our progress was slow because of it. All that first day, I drove through that frigid air, in the middle of what seemed to be nowhere, far from houses or barns or people, picking my way carefully through the deep snow, getting stuck occasionally when, recognizing by the roaring motor I was in trouble, Peter would ride back, dismount, and drive the truck out for me. After three or four rescues, I learned from him how to do it myself. It had been cold when we started out in the morning, but as the day wore on the temperature began to drop and it got colder and colder.

Darkness came in the late afternoon and we hadn't yet reached our destination. The wind had begun to blow, and snow drifted across the backs of the cattle and the hood of the truck and swirled up around the riders hunched on their horses, sometimes blotting them from view. I discovered that if I stayed too close to the back of the herd — they had never "strung out" that day, but moved in a clump — my headlights would throw their own shadows over the cattle, which would frighten them and make them run, bad for their lungs in that intense cold. I tried to keep far enough back to prevent that from happening, but in that directionless, timeless darkness and that inexpressible cold, if I could not see the riders between me and the cattle, I grew frightened. I struggled to keep the truck neither too close nor too far away.

By now it was about thirty below Fahrenheit, completely dark, and we had still not arrived at wherever we were going. Picking my way carefully so as not to get stuck, I shone my headlights on what looked like a safe, flat spot and drove through it only to discover that the level snow hid a deep depression. I was stuck. I shifted into first and tried to roar ahead, and then through neutral into reverse, then back again, till I'd set up a rhythm, the old prairie trick of "rocking" my way out. But we were in too deep, and in a minute I'd stalled the motor. The riders kept moving on into the blackness out of the range of my headlights and were gone from view. Sean and I sat helpless, alone in the stalled, cooling truck in the darkness.

Before I had time to feel fully the fear that was threatening to swamp me, out of that blackness Peter came riding toward us, icicles hanging from his horse's mane and muzzle and clinging to his own eyebrows, lashes and beard. When he saw how deeply we were stuck, he told us to wait and he'd get the four-wheel-drive and pull us out.

"We're there," he added, as he rode away. I peered ahead and, at the place where the truck lights melted softly into moving, black emptiness, I saw a fence corner. How the men had found a mere fence corner, and the right one, in the blackness and blowing snow, I had no idea. I imagine there'd been consultations between them I hadn't heard, about how the fencelines ran in that field and, relative to them, what our location at any moment must be.

Peter was back in a minute in the four-wheel-drive and pulled us out. All the riders but one piled into the two trucks, while Peter and the remaining rider, using the trucks' headlights, held an intense conversation about what to do with the four horses, which were tired, hungry and very cold. The image is forever imprinted in my mind: sitting in the cab of that truck in that black and frigid winter night with snow all around us, far from succor of any kind, watching Peter and the other man unsaddle all but the lead horse, throw the saddles on the back of one of the trucks, and change their bridles for halters.

Then, as we watched, one by one they tied the tails of each of three of the horses to the halter of the horse ahead of it, till there was a line of four horses tied tail to halter, together. The other man mounted the lead horse and leaned down from his saddle to hear better while Peter gave him precise, careful instructions about how to find a ranch house almost three miles away across the frozen fields and through the blowing snow that obliterated landmarks. All of us knew, even I, that if the rider got confused in the darkness, or if the fences which he would be following had been changed from the year before, there was a good chance he might pass that shelter by and freeze to death.

The men closed the gate on the cattle, threw off the feed for them, settled them down for the night in a low spot out of the wind, and we went around by a prairie trail, with Peter driving my truck, to the ranch house where we found our rider had reached safely. The horses had already been fed and stabled, and the woman there invited us in for coffee. Not even trying to hide her surprise and what might have been a touch of awe, she said, "We expected you through one of these days, but we sure didn't think it would be on a night like this."

It was an overwhelming experience which afterward I could hardly find words to describe adequately to my friends and family. My mother must have been alarmed, although she was careful not to say so. Her memories of her hard years in the bush must have been strong, and I think she wanted to advise me to give up the idea of marrying Peter because of the hardship she was sure I would have to endure. On the other hand, if the Butalas were far from rich, having succeeded in wilderness where we had failed, it was clear they had at least a considerably more financially secure life than we had had when we were enduring those years of privation in the bush country, and this would make my life much easier than hers had been. And she must have seen in Peter the same qualities I saw: his strength of character and physical strength, his stability, his integrity and his quiet competence.

The draw was powerful and it was not mitigated by the obvious physical danger of such a life; it may even have been enhanced by it. I saw nobody in my city life doing anything more physically dangerous than walking to work, and in Saskatoon that wasn't much of a risk. I'd had enough of my windowless office at the university and the endless maneuvering for advantage, not to mention the incredibly hard work people of my lowly rank had to do for distressingly low pay; I'd had enough of the men I was meeting, each one of whom seemed to be more insecure, convoluted and uncertain than the last one; I couldn't wait to put it all behind me. The winter cattle drive had been more than memorable — it had been invigorating, simple, firmly tied to a physical reality that I had been missing and, without even realizing it, longing for.

I put my faith in Peter. I was in love. If I was giving up what had turned out to be a fantasy of a closetful of satin ballgowns and the life to go with them, if I was giving up men with doctorates and fancy cars, it was for a second chance at a meaningful life and for a man who clearly was what he appeared to be. I saw myself merely as escaping into a simpler, more pure and more ethical life, a life that made clear sense as the one I was living had ceased to do. Despite the powerful feelings surfacing in me, it really didn't occur to me that when I married I was going into a life in Nature. Nature entered into my picture of my future merely as an unavoidable background, desirable chiefly because of its — oh, unexamined cliché! — peacefulness and beauty.

Peter and I were married in late May, and since there was no new house on either the hay farm or the ranch — where there were only two settlers' shacks pulled together around 1934 and sided over to form one house — for the first two and a half years we moved back and forth between the two places with the cattle and the seasons. It was awkward and sometimes confusing, but I didn't care. There was something freeing about having two "camps," as Peter often called them, instead of one home. And I loved both places despite the fact that both houses were too small, dilapidated and lacking in amenities that for years I'd been able to take for granted. On the hay farm we lived in a log house that had been built there before 1912, though we don't know exactly when or by whom. We had electricity and running water in both places, but no bathrooms, especially no indoor toilets of any kind. Often I had to get up in the middle of the night to go outside to the toilet, something I had done until I was thirteen years old.

In my first year of living that way, rising in the night to go outside, wending my way down a footpath under the stars, sometimes being startled by the distant drumming of horses' hooves growing louder as they approached and by the rush of wind as they swept by me in the darkness, hearing, but not seeing them, I had a dream.

I dreamt it was night and I had stepped outside the door of our log house into the deepest winter. There were mountains of untouched snow everywhere, great high drifts of it banked up around the house to its roof and there were thick, long stalactites of ice hanging from the eaves. I was wearing a nightgown — strangely, the one I wore on my wedding night of my first marriage in 1961, white with white lace trim on the bodice — but I wasn't at all cold.

A white coyote appeared from out of the darkness on my left. It trotted slowly past me only three or four feet away, and as it passed it turned its head to stare straight at me into my eyes. It limped on three paws, holding up its right front paw to its chest as if it had been wounded. Even then, knowing nothing of these things, I knew by the silver-white color of its thick coat that it was a spirit animal. It was clear I was out of the realm of everyday life; I was in an archetypal realm, a limitless, timeless world of pure wilderness.

I cherished the dream and told Peter about it, but what did it mean? I puzzled over it for days without making any progress in its interpretation. I knew nothing about the whole study of dreams, and any significant dreams I'd had before had always involved people and were clearly about problems in my daily life. I knew that this dream was a product of this perfectly unnameable *thing* I felt stirring inside me from the time of that first weekend I'd spent in what became my new home; I recognized the intense, rich mystery and beauty of the dream. I was fascinated and at first could think of little else, but as the months passed, I thought less and less about it, believing that one day its meaning would come to me and in the meantime it was useless to keep puzzling over it.

But the dream caused something else to happen: the memory of a childhood experience came flooding back to me — something that happened when I was eight years old and making my First Communion. We had been told in catechism that, after having been purified by confession and penance, when we received the Host for the first time in our lives, the Holy Spirit, conceived of by the artist in our catechism materials as a shining white dove, would enter us.

I had — sometimes I think I was born with — a powerful sense of myself as a sinner, as unworthy, as always guilty, which a Catholic upbringing presumably did nothing to alleviate, and the source of which, though I have some glimmerings of it, will remain untold on these pages. But I was, in the way of children, especially those kept close to their mothers, an innocent. I believed what I was told; I believed it with all my heart, wholly, without question.

In my new white dress, white stockings, shoes and veil, I knelt at the altar of that small wooden church on the edge of the town, surrounded by wild grass and beyond that by wheatfields. The priest approached and, murmuring a prayer in Latin, put the Host on my tongue. I rose with the other children and began the walk back to the pew where my parents and sisters waited. And then I felt it: something, though this was all so many years ago I barely remember, but something I perceived as a cloud of white light lit inside my chest, swelling till it filled it.

But those words fail to give the miraculous sense of it. It was *not myself*, it was both within me and bigger than me; it was, when I tried to tell my mother after as we waited in the car for our father to come from his chat with the priest and drive us home to Sunday dinner, as if the Holy Ghost had come as was foretold and filled me with its whiteness and purity. I had no idea beyond that white dove, what the Holy Spirit the priest talked about was. If I was merely incarnating the priest's description through the power of his suggestion, I had forgotten the rushing of wings, the cooing, the wind.

My mother was an unwilling Catholic, having converted from Anglicanism to marry our father. "You're only lightheaded from fasting," she snapped angrily, wanting, I suppose, nothing to do with pagan Catholicism, and detesting seeing it in her own child. Or, given her background, perhaps it merely struck her as unutterably vulgar.

Yet both of these, the dream and the numinous experience of my First Communion, served to remind me of another puzzling yet profoundly moving dream — if indeed it was a dream; vision better describes it — I had had at another significant moment in my life, this one three months after the birth of my only child.

In the early evening I had gone into the bedroom to try to catch up on my sleep. I lay down, closed my eyes, and then I was transported into the same realm that all these years later I had visited in my dream of the white coyote. There was my infant son asleep in his carriage where I put him each day, in the backyard of the house where we lived in the small town where I had taken a job teaching school. The carriage was sitting on the grass. Beside it a narrow cement sidewalk ran from the gate into the yard to the kitchen door. Everything was as it was in real life, including the tall old poplar trees that formed a border around the small yard. In the dream nothing happened, nothing moved or changed. The child slept on, motionless, lost in his infant world.

What was extraordinary was that I saw clearly, indisputably, finally, that the child, the grass, the trees, the sky above were all woven of the same material, were all part of the same fabric, which was the fabric of which the universe is made, and that this fabric *lived*. As pointed contrast, the cement sidewalk lay ugly and dead, a scar in the picture; except for it, the whole scene was transcendent with beauty, the colors had an intensity, a purity not present in real life, and the dream was imbued with a feeling of the perfect peace and benevolence of the universe.

I came to myself and the darkened bedroom, the furniture bulky shadows along the walls, an arrow of light below the door into the next room. Bewildered, I called my husband and asked him how long I'd been asleep. "A half hour or so," he said. "Why?" I told him about my dream. "If it was a dream," I said. Then, "I don't think it was a dream."

I had to understand what had happened to me. My husband thought he knew, having read about just such experiences. He found a book — at least, I think this was what happened — by an important East Indian philosopher — Radakrishnan? Krishnamurti? Or was it someone else? I no longer remember — which described this very experience, calling it "Universal Oneness," and endeavored to explain what it meant. I looked further and found that experiences having just the characteristics of mine had been recorded over and over again in cultures around the world. It seemed that in Eastern philosophies/religions, at least, it was the basic vision of the universe, the deepest and most meaningful spiritual experience one might have.

Even though all these descriptions in books validated it intellectually and gave me interpretations to mull over with awe, what little I understood of the vision was the ambience that permeated it. Meaning had not been given to me in words and the words I was reading seemed trivial and disconnected in the face of the magnitude and beauty of the vision itself. All I really knew was that I had been given an insight of profound importance, but read about it as I did, it was one I couldn't make sense of in a personal way. Although I was sure it should, I couldn't figure out how it was supposed to affect my life.

For days nothing in the real world looked the same. Every fork on the table, every bar of sunlight slanting across a room, the eyebrows and lashes of my baby seemed more beautiful and more puzzling, and yet more real than I had dreamt or imagined. All this *meant* something, it seemed, something I had never guessed, had never conceived of myself or been told of by priests or teachers or had read in books. The world was deeper and more baffling than I knew, but how I should fit this vision into my life, I had no idea.

For long periods of time after that I didn't think of it at all, but every once in a while in the many intervening years between its occurrence and my marriage to Peter, it would come back to me and I would once again puzzle over it. I had relegated it to the realm of never-to-be-solved and seldom-remembered mysteries, when the dream of the spirit coyote brought it back to me with something of its long-lost, original force. So many years had passed, fourteen or so, and I still didn't understand. Yet, in pondering these dream-visions — the white cloud, the spirit coyote, the dream of universal oneness — I saw that in the latter two I had returned to my archetypal world, the world of my first introduction to this star-ridden, green and scented universe, to the world children inhabit — innocent even in its danger, edenlike in its dark, rich beauty. Puzzling over them, surrounded as I was by miles of prairie still in the state it had been in since the glaciers had melted back ten thousand years before, with mirages hovering in the distance, the nights filled with the distant wail of coyotes, and with the canopy of stars, and the wind a constant, whispering companion, I began to have the first intimations that there was in Nature much more than met the eye, something that existed in back of it. I did not know what that something was, I didn't even expect ever to know, but nevertheless I strained every day to catch a glimpse of it. I thought if I could just see it, maybe I would understand it and that understanding would show me how to live.

I was so overwhelmed by the dream of the spirit coyote that more than a dozen years later, when I had become a writer, I gave it to Amy Sparrow, the heroine of my novel *The Fourth Archangel*. I was trying to express something; I am still trying to say it, which means to understand it. This book is my response to that emissary of Nature, the dream coyote, and to what I think was his message to me, for through understanding his message I might also come to know what the larger vision I had had as a young mother meant.

BELONGING

Often at the ranch Peter would get up at dawn, catch one of the saddle horses in the corral, groom it, give it hay, and come in for breakfast while his horse fed. Then he'd saddle it and ride off into the fields for a day of looking for calves which had lost their mothers or vice versa, for mix-ups of various kinds, for illness or accidents, and inspecting fences and water-holes and the state of the grass in each field. It was not unusual, during those summer days of seemingly endless light, for me not to see him again till darkness had crept up the hillsides, turning them black against the luminous night sky. His father and mother had told me, each in their own way, not to worry when he didn't return: his father sagaciously, "This is the way of cattlemen, of cowboys"; his mother wryly, "They always come back eventually, none the worse for wear."

When the other women of the community were visiting each other, I knew nobody; while they were raising children, I had no young children left at home; while they were growing gardens and preserving food, I had few people to cook for, no garden yet, and the tiniest of houses which took no time to look after; while they were sometimes driving to part-time jobs, there was no real need for me to get a job and we lived so far from the nearest town that any full-time work was impracticable; while they were driving tractors and farm trucks and occasionally running to town for parts, Peter, used to doing everything himself or with hired help, didn't ask me to help, at least partly because I didn't know how. At the advanced age of thirty-six I was just learning to ride a horse.

I began to go for walks. Sometimes I would carry a lunch out to where I knew I would find Peter and the hired man fencing, or I would walk the fenceline to where the herd of horses were grazing and spend half an hour talking to them across the fence till they grew bored with my company and wandered away. I would walk to the places I had seen from the truck where the view was especially distant or beautiful and sit on the stiff, dry, prairie grass and try to assimilate the stunning, bare sweep of land.

East of the house about a mile was one of the highest hills on the ranch — you can see its silhouette blue against the horizon from miles away — and in those early days before I dared to venture too far from the house and yard I sometimes chose it for my destination. More than once from the crown of that hill I'd spotted Peter on horseback, a black stroke against the yellow grass a mile or two away, moving slowly among the cattle, disappearing almost at once between hills. If I felt lonely I'd sometimes walk out and climb that hill in hopes of catching a reassuring glimpse of him.

On a hot summer afternoon, having been alone since dawn and bored with the pursuits I'd been toying with for the last few hours, I wandered out to that hilltop, my head down, thinking. In those early days, as my old life began to waver and dissolve and the new one still had no firm shape, I was always deep in thought.

The side I was approaching the hill from slopes gradually up to the crest; on the other side it drops off abruptly a hundred or so feet to the prairie below where the spring run-off sometimes pools to form a shallow slough. By this time of the year, July, the water had long since evaporated, but it had left behind a stand of grass richer than the surrounding prairie, where there were always a few animals to be found.

On that day, on the far side of the hill in that slough-bottom, twenty or so cows stood grazing or lay with their calves beside them peacefully chewing their cuds. In their midst Peter's saddle horse, reins dragging, browsed lazily too. And far off at the edge of the cluster of cattle, a couple of antelope stood, noses down in the grass. All of them were oblivious to my presence and paying no attention to each other, as if they were all members of the same contented tribe on that still, hot afternoon, under that magnificent dome of sky, and in the midst of those thousands of acres of short, pale grass. About a hundred feet out from the foot of the hill, in the midst of his animals, lying facedown in the grass, head on one bent arm, hat shielding his eyes, Peter lay sound asleep.

I stopped dead in my tracks, overcome with an emotion I couldn't identify: that I had caught him in a moment so private I felt I had no right to be there; that something was happening here that was beyond my experience and my understanding, but that meant something — something significant; I could feel it in my heart and in my gut — which my brain couldn't grasp, couldn't name or classify.

I backed away quickly before I was seen; I hurried down the long slope of the hill and full of silent wonder walked back across the fields to the house. I never breathed a word of what I had seen to anyone.

On her deathbed our mother had dreamt, she told us, that she was back on the farm in Manitoba and the five of us were little girls again. We were in the summer kitchen, she said, and outside it was raining. A tent was pitched in the yard and a family of children were in it. The five of us were begging her to let them into the house with us, but she wouldn't because, she said, they'd track in mud and she had just washed the floor. "I should have let them in," she said, terribly upset, as if it had really happened and wasn't just a dream. "I should have let them in. I shouldn't have worried about the mud."

I knew at once it was a dream about how she had watched us too closely, how she had held firm in her determination to protect us from a world she was herself afraid of, and how she now saw she had been wrong. I grew up timid and afraid of the world as a result of this watch-fulness, and any need I had for adventure I had always stifled or fulfilled vicariously. Now, in my only act of real daring, I had turned away from the world I'd been raised for and understood, had thrown away every-thing I had worked for, in favor of a world about which I knew nothing and the promise of which I couldn't even read.

If I had had stirrings of memories powerful enough to draw me back into the natural world in which I had spent my first years, I was mistaken if I thought I knew anything factual about how to make a living in it, or even how to live in it as my husband did. Whatever it was or would be, I had not imagined beforehand, and even though I was now living in it, it was an uneasy kind of living, laden with a sense of waiting, of discovery and possibility, but without any firm shape or structure. In the back of my mind I must have thought that only the form and the daily activities would be different than my old life, that the mental and emotional tex-ture, the fabric of it, would be just the same. Not having any experience as an adult of any other way of apprehending and of being in life, how could I imagine it in advance? Or expect it? Or prepare for it?

In the city I had had an identity, or rather several identities: divorcée, single parent, career woman, graduate student, future academic. If the day-to-day living of it was hard, and it was sometimes terribly so, as any single working mother will tell you, it had had its rewards, chiefly that, having gone from the daughter of a rather strict and formidable mother (at least I found her so although my sisters, I think, would describe her otherwise) to the wife of a man I had somehow wound up trying to please but never could, I had had for the first time in my life a degree of personal autonomy. I earned my own money and could do with it as I chose; I could paint the walls of my house any color I liked; I could cook food I wanted to eat; I could invite over whomever I chose.

At first after my divorce I realized that I had been so demoralized over the years that I didn't even know what color I might want for my walls, or what I liked best to eat, or whom I wanted for friends, or even what kind of a person I was. But as I slowly recovered from the wounds of my marriage and the trauma of its end, these matters gradually began to fall into place. I had begun to remember the person I'd once been, or was becoming, since I was only twenty-one the day I married. I had begun to remember myself as competent, with certain gifts: I had been a visual artist, a good student, a woman who loved to dance. I had been someone who was capable and who had certain dreams of her own of what her life might one day become.

I had, too, a community I knew well and a place in it. I had lived altogether seventeen years in Saskatoon and I knew its corners, its ins and outs thoroughly. Everywhere I looked I saw familiar faces, people I saw on the street every day, even when I had no names for them. I had spent a total of nine years on the university campus and could remember when it had had only two thousand students and half the buildings it had when I left. I was a member of a large family, with cousins in the city, and nieces and nephews, and not far away aunts and uncles on both my mother's and father's sides, and until their deaths, grandparents too. I had never been without that sense of being part of a family, not even when I'd lived in other provinces; it was not something I'd ever given a thought to.

It's true, though, that I often found the day-to-day living of this life of freedom in many ways terribly hard. I had been raised expecting to be supported by a man and had been trained to be a good wife and mother. Although I'd always worked, I'd never before felt the real burden to succeed in order to support my family in quite the way men do, as a burden they are raised to shoulder, even do with some pride and eagerness. In my career I had to learn all the skills men are so good at, like taking full responsibility, standing up for myself, expecting without thought to take care of myself and my child.

Still, the benefits seemed to me to outweigh the problems, and the most wonderful benefit of all was my women friends. I'd been one of a group, some of whom I'd known for twenty years and others whom I'd just met, who were companions, confidantes, intellectual peers, colleagues, people to go to parties with and plays, concerts, movies and for walks in the park, to eat lunch with, to have over for dinner and who had me to their houses, women to whom I could go, and they to me, when we had to talk to someone, with whom we would trust our deepest secrets. My dearest friends from those days are still my dearest friends, even though they are scattered across the country now, and I see each of them perhaps once a year. Together we were inventing a new world, and that resulted in ties so deep to each other that they'll never be broken in this life.

We were part of the ferment of the new wave of feminism that had risen in the sixties and peaked in the seventies. We were meeting in consciousness-raising groups, whether formally constituted as such or not; we were speaking to each other, for most of us for the first time, as sisters, even though we were not blood relatives and often not even intimate friends. We were breaking down some of the barriers that had existed between individual women as far back as we could remember or had heard about from our mothers, and were seeing that we were a race, a tribe, a nation of people, when we had thought each of us belonged to our mothers and to men.

We were exploring womanhood too, well beyond the stereotypes we'd been raised in: what it is to be female, to be wives and mothers, to approach the world as female beings. We were searching for and finding our power through deliberately trying to tear down the walls of fear society, we had believed, had forced us to erect between us.

So our friendships were wider, deeper, and there were more of them than most of us, at least of my age, had had since we'd graduated from high school and left childhood behind. They also held a more important place in the lives of each one of us. We supported each other at work and in our private lives; it sometimes seems to me that we lived in a sense collectively. It was, I see now, a wonderful time to be a woman, even though what united us primarily, beyond our femaleness, were our common struggles and suffering in a time when, on the one hand, we were being told and telling each other that women could do and be anything we wanted, and on the other, nobody was admitting how very hard that was turning out to be.

But we were also having a lot of fun; it seemed every weekend one of us gave a party where we danced and talked and ate and danced some more, not going home till the sun was rising. We were nearly all divorced, separated or otherwise unmarried, many of us products of the fifties with our overdeveloped superegos, and in our newfound feminism we were experiencing for the first time in our lives a sense that there were endless possibilities to our own lives, not just the single, precise picture we'd been raised to believe was the only possibility: a husband, several children, a house, a car, a lawn to mow, rugs to vacuum, dishes to wash. Although men were also present, it was understood that their presence was great but not necessary, and that we were a gang, not a group of couples, for we were realizing that — oh, most amazing fact of all — we could have fun with each other and as a group, we didn't have to wait around till an individual man invited us. And that realization alone gave us back some of the power we'd lost.

All of this is to say that my women friends had become so firmly woven into the fabric of my life that they were as vital to me as breathing, that I knew I would miss them as much as I would miss the blood sisters I was leaving behind. It also meant that I took it for granted that in time I'd find a new set of women friends with whom I could share my life in the same way I had with my friends in the city, and so I approached the women I was meeting in my new community blithely, eagerly, wholly unaware that things worked differently in the country.

One of the things which I am constantly having to correct people about is the urban perception that rural life is the same whether it's small-town life, or farm or ranch life. Farm life is very different from ranch life although there are similarities, especially for people who do mixed farming. But on a true ranch the primary business is the care and feeding of cattle, big herds of them, who lead a semi-wild life out on the range and whose care necessitates for the ranchers a life lived out in the wilderness in all kinds of weather, and it is true, the worse the weather, the more the cattle need you. Farming means growing grain and that is a spring-to-fall job with a free winter, and it takes place on land that, by definition, is no longer wilderness.

Also, when urban people want to describe me as living in Eastend I always correct them, pointing out that I live out in the country. This distinction appears to seem to them irritatingly trivial, as if I am merely nitpicking. But town life, too, is a different kettle of fish than true country life.

Because I'd never lived on a farm before, and because Peter's main interest and daily work wasn't farming, often I didn't understand even the simplest remarks about what everybody's husband was up to at the moment, much less could I contribute any of my own. Not that it would have been any easier if the women were all married to ranchers, since ranch women tend to be horsewomen, real outdoorswomen, with the same practised eye for cattle as the men, and many of the same hard-earned skills, none of which I had or, to be truthful, wanted very badly.

How the women worked! I'd never seen anything like it. They kept enormous gardens and canned or pickled or froze everything in them, often at the same time as harvest when they had a crew of men, albeit a tiny one compared to the days of threshing crews, to cook for; they knew how to handle every piece of meat from a side of beef, even how to can it, as well as lamb and pork, and how each had to be butchered although the men did the butchering. They understood the mysteries of keeping a milk cow, milking her and using the separator and cleaning it, and raising chicks up to chickens without the coyotes getting them, and of gathering the eggs without being pecked; they could make cottage cheese and headcheese and it wasn't uncommon to make an angel food cake from scratch. In a country where bakeries were either too far away or not much good they made all their own bread; they could and did run the farm machinery and haying equipment, and did all this while driving the boys to hockey practice and the girls to skating lessons and music lessons and a thousand and one extracurricular activities at the school; they nearly all had their hobbies, chiefly handicrafts, and they all did community work besides, in fact, were the organizing force that kept rural communities alive. Beside them I felt like an incompetent idiot, and the longer I knew them, the less I thought that traditional women had it easier than the new breed of urban career mothers. They had husbands, that was all, who presumably, if they did not share the work, then at least provided moral support and companionship.

My own growing sense of inferiority to these marvelous women, combined with a lack of desire to be like them, since I knew I would drop down dead at the end of one day like every one of theirs, and also because I believed something was missing from their lives that I had myself and didn't want to lose (even though, if asked, I wouldn't have been able to say what it was) also got in the way of friendships. Well, I told myself, true friendship takes time to build; I can wait.

That some of the difficulty had nothing to do with me as a person was brought home to me when I asked a woman my own age, who seemed to me subtly different from the others in the room at the time, how long she'd lived in the district. "Twenty years," she said, and sighed. I had been in the community a dozen years when a woman, listing members of the community for some reason I've forgotten now, remarked to me that she'd left out a certain family. "They didn't move here till the forties," she said, "so I never think of them." She meant that even though that family had lived here for almost fifty years, in her estimation, they would never be truly local people. By that time I was the one to sigh.

When I first came here to live, country people were country people to me; big farmers, small farmers, it was all the same to me. I didn't know the basic fact that there's a social hierarchy out here, too, or of what it consisted. Although in a strange way the class system I was familiar with — based on income, visible affluence, education, job type, whether manual labor, blue collar or professional, and to a small degree, family background, as well as whatever else urban sociologists are arguing about these days — didn't entirely hold, there was indubitably a class system at work.

This was a world which at first appeared to me to be nearly all working class, where education wasn't particularly valued since you could be a well-educated bad farmer or a poorly educated top-notch farmer, where differences in jobs were minimal, and where having leisure time wasn't especially desirable — too many farmers lost interest in life when they retired, sometimes turning to alcohol for consolation, or suffering a heart attack suddenly and dying. Yet there were still the aristocrats, plebeians and untouchables, and the trick was to figure out which was which and why.

Land springs to mind at once, for with land comes money, and wealth is certainly a measure of class in both town and country. Yet, when people began to buy more land regardless of the escalating prices, Peter, who had no shortage of land, would quote to me the old Russian dictum, "How much land does a man need?" which his Slovakian father, who'd arrived penniless in this country in 1913, used to quote to him, and the answer to which is, "Six feet to bury him."

But to say land is the basis of the class system is to give an inadequate description of the situation. At least as important is the length of residence of a family in the country. "In the country" means in any particular district. Such is the degree of pride in this that I'm told there is in Maple Creek an organization which holds an annual dinner which may be attended only by those whose families have been in the country a hundred years or more. And even I, I confess, am proud of being able to say that my Manitoba relatives still live on farms established by their families in 1884 and 1885. That my Québécois and Acadian relatives have been in Canada since the mid-seventeenth century counts for less out here than the other.

But as a caveat to the above, to earn respect within this system of landownership and length of residence, a holdover, I think, from pioneering days when all the work was manual, it is also essential to have a reputation for being a hard worker. A man could be a drunk, a wife-abuser, a fighter, I used to tell Peter indignantly, but if he worked hard every day, nonetheless, other men respected him. In fact, it seems to me that that ethic, basic to the besieged rural value system, was the one most in need of revamping to meet a modern agricultural society, and yet was one of the most basic strands to its unraveling fabric.

I learned to be constantly aware of the amount of work accomplished by others. If I felt that in this something was puzzlingly out of sync with reality as I knew it, I still couldn't help but notice that if the men worked hard, it was evident to me that they hadn't a patch on the women, whose work never ended. As an extreme example, one woman told me angrily after she'd — temporarily, it turned out — left her husband: "I work all day out in the field with him and when it's mealtime I come in and cook it while he sits with his feet up and reads the paper."

Eventually, after more than a dozen years, I could see that the reasons for the way people were treated by other community members were frequently things I would never know because they had happened two generations back, or in childhood, or had nothing to do with anybody living today. They were so embedded in the fabric of the community that they could never be teased out, and the people who were responding to them didn't even notice anymore, or never had noticed, that they were. And I, a stranger, would be years in learning what they were, if I ever did at all.

Truly belonging to the community of women in the way I'd belonged to my community in the city was going to be much harder than I'd thought. I still didn't understand that I would never have the conversations with my rural women friends that I had had with my urban friends. I would never have them because not just the daily round of activity but the approach to life, the view of it, was utterly different.

In time I was invited to join clubs whose work, unfortunately, I wasn't interested in, so that after debating with myself, and much as I wanted to belong, I declined. To this day, no matter how it has been here or how lonely I have been at times, I don't regret declining. I longed to belong, but without realizing it I was resisting. Although I hadn't yet figured it out rationally and was acting strictly from the gut, I had enough presence of mind in this case to follow my intuition which said that there was no choice involved; belonging would have to be on my own terms, whatever I might finally discover those terms to be.

Many of us have childhood dreams that are unfulfilled and that we carry with us for life. Mine was to be a visual artist. Despite the fact that my two undergraduate majors were art and English literature, so complete was my rejection of what I now know to be my true nature that when I returned to the university after ten years away in the work force I had deliberately chosen to do a master's degree in the Education of Exceptional Children. This was how I had made my living for the previous seven or eight years, and when I had decided to go back to university, I'd rejected doing a master's degree in art because — it was the early seventies — it seemed to me that fine arts departments had fallen into such chaos that a Virgoish person like myself would be driven crazy in one. I rejected doing a master's degree in English because I thought after all those years of working first with street kids in Halifax and then developmentally delayed teenagers in Saskatoon the sheer boredom of nitpicking over words would be the death of me. At the time I really believed these were the true reasons, and looking back now, I can only add that it is just possible that I refused both courses not only because making a living would be so precarious after but, more than that, because I so loved both fields that I was deeply afraid of failure in them.

From the time I started school as a six-year-old, I'd known I could draw and that drawing and painting gave me great pleasure. As the years of my life as a schoolchild passed, this skill or talent was reinforced over and over again by both my classmates and my teachers, and was cherished at home by our mother. (My sisters were also gifted in this way, my older sister much more than I.) Often I could draw better than anyone else in my class, and I loved art more — though I loathed crafts, which were what art classes more often consisted of and at which I was very bad. I had begun to imagine a life as an artist for myself.

I reached high school and although I attended the high school where the children of the working class and the immigrants went, from which you could graduate already a secretary or a mechanic, by some fluke I've never understood, it was at the time the only school in the city with a full-fledged art program and a genuine artist as department head and the only teacher. I was able to major in art, and to have my thirst for it constantly tended to by my daily classes with him through most of my four years there.

My art teacher (and also my older sister's) was the well-known Saskatchewan artist Ernest Lindner, and as an immigrant himself he understood that those of us who faced the future without financial security or useful contacts needed to be given confidence, needed to be told that even working-class kids had a right to a fulfilling life, that even I might go to university and take a degree in art, which, armed with his certainty that I could, I eventually did.

I had finished the first year of my B.A. majoring in art when I began to worry about making a living. I had had no other plans, no other alternatives in mind but becoming an artist. Now I began to face the fact of the struggle artists' lives are for mere survival, and I knew I did not want to spend the rest of my life in poverty. I had had enough of that — or so I told myself. Now I think that I was simply afraid that I wasn't talented enough, that I simply hadn't the guts to strike out in the world without a sure way of making a living.

At the end of my first year I switched into education, received my B.Ed. at the end of four years — I'd already been married for a year — and stayed on for one more year to finish my B.A., still majoring in art. I would be a teacher of high school English, and if anybody would let me, I'd teach art, as a rather pitiful substitute for a life as a genuine artist.

After that the inevitable happened — nobody wanted an art teacher. I was so busy working and, by then, being a mother that I had no time anymore to paint, and before I knew it, my self-identification as an artist had faded away to a pale and almost forgotten shadow of its former self. I barely had time to mourn it. Except for my paintings hanging on the walls of our various apartments, no one would ever have known that was who I had once been. Deeply buried though, deeper and deeper with each passing year, was that budding artist inside me. I always believed, without ever really thinking about it, that one day I would return to my art.

Six or so years into our marriage which, although I didn't fully comprehend this at the time, wasn't going very well, during one of our many moves from one apartment to another, my husband threw in the city dump the dozen or so paintings I had kept as proof I'd once been an artist. It was several weeks before I even knew about it; there was then no hope of ever getting them back. I didn't even look for them.

I was too stunned by this act even to express to him my shock. I'd expressed more anger to him for losing my place in a book. I said virtually nothing; not then, not since. And I didn't mean to let it matter; I thought if I didn't let it, it wouldn't. I didn't know that there is a place deep inside where one's real life goes on, much like an underground river in parched, dry country, which flows whether one knows about it or not. Although it was such a blow I couldn't even respond, having been knocked to my knees metaphorically, it was a blow that I would eventually find had nonetheless left a lasting wound.

It is worth mentioning, I think, that I long ago forgave my young husband for this act, not because I am a saint, but because neither one of us understood our own lives then, and had he understood its significance to me, I know he would not have done it. To this day I'm not sure how I repaid this wound, but I know it had to have been something just as terrible, and in just as uncomprehending a way.

During the last year of my city life, after Peter and I decided to marry, but before the ceremony, the way I spent my leisure time had begun to change. For years I had read only in my field, trying desperately to keep up. Now I went back to reading novels, something I hadn't had time to do for years, even though reading had been, from the moment I learned how in the convent on the banks of the Saskatchewan River so long ago, the single most important activity in my life. It was as if, knowing that the end of my long travail at the university was in sight, I was slowly rediscovering the interests I'd abandoned one by one, mostly out of sheer exhaustion, over the previous years.

I took up needlework and made a couple of extremely ugly appliquéd cushion covers. I did some crewelwork and considered, but didn't get around to doing, batik, which I'd learned during a couple of years when I'd taught some elementary school classes in art. I began to realize slowly and with increasing eagerness that the long-awaited day had finally arrived: after the wedding and my move to the ranch, I would once again take up painting.

I arrived in my new life equipped with soft-leaded pencils and thick, rough paper, intending to find my way slowly by honing my drawing skills first. Of course, there were the inevitable physical hardships that initially took much of my energy, but eventually even those became, if not routine, at least manageable. Afternoons, when Peter was off riding by himself or working with other men, or doing business on occasions when I couldn't accompany him, I planned to take out my drawing pad and pencils and go looking for subjects. And I tried to.

I carried my equipment out to the corral and made a few desultory attempts at rendering the barn with its interesting, half-broken cupola full of swallows. I tried the weeds growing up around the weathered bottom rail of the corral, and the rough shacks that had once been bunkhouses or settlers' cabins and now held the detritus of settlers' lives such as worn, stiffened buffalo coats, broken kerosene lamps, nicked and crushed blue granite pots, rickety tables and rusty iron bedframes; I struggled to render the old hand waterpump on its cracked wooden platform. At the stockyards in a nearby town, while Peter attended a cattle sale, I sat in the truck and drew the town's huge grain elevator and its annex. It is the only drawing I completed.

Something was missing. The first few pencil strokes had taught me that I'd lost nearly all my craft in the last twenty or so years. I was not really worried about that; I knew I could get that back. What was missing was something more essential than mere learned technique. Drawing takes intense concentration, a complete absorption in the subject and in the materials one is working with. This is usually a fully joyous kind of concentration — at least it had always been for me.

Now I found I couldn't concentrate at all, couldn't find that level of absorption, could not for the life of me dredge up desire anymore. I had thought naively in my new life I would go back to being a painter, and now I had to accept that that dream was over, that I would never paint again. I had lost the heart for it. I was devastated.

I was still an urban person; I came from a world where everyone was defined precisely by what he or she did. With no job, no friends, no family, *nothing to do,* I began to search for an anchor, or a framework, a shape, in which to live out my days in this strange, new world which unexpectedly was, at least on a day-to-day level, as alien to me as if I'd married an Arab or an Inuit and gone to live in his culture.

The afternoon I walked out into the field, climbed the hill and saw Peter asleep on the ground with his animals was a deeply significant moment for me, a benchmark against which I measured each of my new experiences. It seemed to me that something had been revealed to me about my new husband that I had never guessed at, that I had seen a glimmer of something about my new life that would inform and instruct me if I could just understand it. The moment was like my dream-visions in that whatever its significance was, I *felt* it rather than verbalized it or assimilated it intellectually. Like the childhood morning when my chest had filled with light, my entire body felt what I was seeing not like a blow but more like opening the door of a dark, gloomy house onto the outdoor world of light and warmth and color. I filed this experience away, too, as I had the visions of the spirit coyote, and of the wonder and beauty of the universe. I didn't speak of them, but this did not mean I'd forgotten them.

In secrecy I pondered and pondered over Peter asleep on the grass among the animals, wondering what it meant, feeling that there was, just out of my grasp, a message that once deciphered would be the key to understanding my new world which in turn would provide the foundation I was missing, that would show me what to do with the long hours of my days, the ways in which I might begin to think about this new world and how to live in it. For I was beginning to see that this new world I'd come to live in was different from my old one, not because of education, class or social structure, but because of whatever it was I had seen that so moved and troubled me the day I'd found Peter asleep in the grass among his animals.

RIDING AND WALKING

If I had no job to go to, no friends I could telephone when I felt lonely, no child to fuss over, if I could not draw or paint, there was always Peter and his work to watch and learn about. Peter was an old-fashioned rancher in that he still did as much of his work as he could on horseback. In the first years of our marriage, trying hard to learn what he and his neighbors actually did all day and how they did it, and why, I asked question after question the way a four-year-old does. His fund of knowledge about the prairie and about ranching was inexhaustible and he enjoyed explaining things to me. By the second year I had begun to record my experiences in a journal.

I rode with Peter in the early years in the truck most of the time, and very often when he went out on horseback, I went too. I wanted very much to learn to ride at least competently, but I wasn't that young anymore; I had never been athletic, and having been on a horse only once or twice before in my life, I was more than a little afraid of them.

If all of that wasn't enough to contend with, I had the additional handicap of being barely five feet tall. Bridling one of Peter's big, none-

too-amenable American Saddlers myself was impossible, and getting off
and on my horse without help or a feed trough or hay bale to stand on
was a challenge. Peter taught me to mount as he did, from beside the
horse's head, facing toward his rump, keeping the reins short and toward
me, and turning the stirrup toward me, which is how bronc riders mount
in order to avoid getting kicked or, should the horse take it into his head
to run, to avoid being dragged. To this day this is the only way I can get
on the quietest horse.

Our daily rides were usually a couple of hours, but often they were six
or eight and sometimes even ten. Naturally, during such long rides, I had
to get off my horse. Dismounting, I slipped my feet out of the stirrups,
held on to the saddle and jumped like an Olympic equestrian does from
an English saddle, but in order to remount in the field, I had to learn to
position my horse in a hollow while I mounted from the high side, or to
put him up against a rock so I had something to stand on.

Peter felt it part of his duties as a husband to catch, bridle and saddle my
horse for me, but being by nature laconic he didn't try to instruct me ver-
bally about how to ride. He believed, as he told me when I asked for instruction, that the best way to learn was as he had as a child: to ride till you were
tired out and then, because it was the most comfortable, your body would
naturally fall into the right way. I had doubts then and I still do.

But all these difficulties seemed less important once we were saddled and
riding together in some far field. Without roads, miles from not only houses
but even power lines or telephone poles, from all signs of human presence,
I forgot my fears and even my aches retreated into the background.

Now the cattle drive I had taken part in before our marriage that had
so frightened and exhilarated me became part of my yearly routine too.
Every winter we moved the cattle the forty miles from the ranch where
there was no shelter or feed supply, to the hay farm where, along the
breaks of the Frenchman River and against the main irrigation canals,
there was plenty of shelter and a winter's supply of food. As the Butala
family had been doing since they'd bought the hay farm in 1949, every

spring we moved them back again to the summer pasture — the ranch — where they stayed seven or eight months.

These were times I learned to both look forward to and to dread — dread because we never knew what we might run into. We've moved in the midst of blizzards, extreme cold when the temperatures dropped to forty and even fifty below Fahrenheit (about the same in Celsius), when it rose to plus fifty Fahrenheit (plus ten Celsius) in January so that the cattle were slogging reluctantly through mud, and were so confused by the unseasonable weather that they kept wanting to turn around and go back to the ranch as if it were spring — and that was worse even than fifty below. One year we moved in snow so deep that because I couldn't handle the truck without getting stuck every two minutes Peter drove and I led his horse, since I didn't dare ride him. I lost five pounds in one day. We moved in spring winds which were so strong and cold that we actually wore two parkas, one on top of the other to keep warm. There was also the wrath of farmers to contend with, a historic hatred of an opposing way of life sometimes so strong that some of them didn't like cattle even to walk down the road past their farms, much less cross their unseeded, frozen land.

The spring we married, the cattle had already been moved. It was not until the next spring, the second year of our marriage, that Peter and I became the typical rancher husband-and-wife team. I'd done the truck driving the first couple of days while Peter and others rode, until we'd gotten the cattle within a few miles of the field where we wanted them, at which point all our help went back home to their own chores. Peter and I were left to bring the herd the rest of the way. We also had to go back several miles to pick up several cows which had calved on the way and been left behind because their newborns couldn't yet travel.

We set out from the ranch at daybreak in zero degree Celsius temperature, with a strong wind blowing and the occasional patter of rain mixed with snow. We rode all day, with only a chunk of cheese to eat and a couple of apples I'd stuffed in my pockets. Together we rounded up most of the cattle in fields as big as six or seven sections, six and more square miles, the size of which exhausted me, especially since the terrain was hill after hill, many a good hundred feet high, but which Peter was rather disdainful about. He'd been raised in a time when from late fall to about the first of May there were open herd laws. This meant he and his father and their hired men rode out each day to herd cattle which were often twenty or more miles away from the barn where they'd saddled their horses.

We brought the cattle down the fireguards plowed in the grass — these are the only roads in such big fields — which curved around the bases of the hills. When we reached a fence corner where there was a gate into the next field, Peter left me to hold the herd while he rode back to the far corners of the field to pick up strays. In each field he was gone a couple of hours, and since there was nobody around but me to make the cattle nervous, and since we'd moved them slowly and quietly, as real cowboys do, without shouting or needlessly running them, and they knew they were going home, they stood patiently enough, or moved out short distances to graze. I was free then to sit on a grassy hilltop from which I could see them all, hold my horse's reins, and wait for his return.

We were, in various directions, from five to ten miles from the nearest inhabited building. There was nobody else in the field; all the days we rode out there we didn't see another person, nor any motorized vehicle. It was cold, nasty weather, but I was warmly dressed and I was learning the art of keeping warm: simple things, like staying in the lee of a hill out of the wind and, where there was no hill, like deer and antelope, lying on the ground in tall grass where it was warm and still, or getting off my horse, positioning him between me and the wind, and walking till my feet were warm. Alone, I'd lie on my back in the grass and watch the clouds, or pluck a handful of grass and let the wind carry it away. I remember, when I was supposed to be herding, lying with my hands under me to keep them warm, my face to the sky, while small, dry snowflakes drifted down on me, and falling asleep on a lonely hill lost in a vast sea of grassy yellow, snow-mottled hills.

I was never bored; the time passed unnoticed. I think I must have been absorbing the atmosphere and the feel of Nature because I wasn't studying anything in particular, not the grasses, not the few birds' nests we found, not the horned larks or the hawks or the eagles or the antelope we saw. I was just being there at a time in my life when I could be still and in the present, because my new life was so full of strange and compelling experiences in need of being assimilated that I had little thought of the future.

I rode with Peter that spring bringing the cattle home for, my journal says, one six-hour and three nine-hour days. On the morning of the fifth day, after we'd breakfasted and the horses were saddled and waiting in the barn, I had on my outdoor clothes and was about to pull on my second boot, I said to Peter, "I can't go." I was exhausted, too tired even to find the strength to pull on that second boot. Peter rode that day, the last before the cattle reached home, without me. The entry in my new journal — one of the first I made — ends: *It's five o'clock, Peter's not back yet, and I'm still tired.* I was tired for days.

Every spring for perhaps the first five years of our marriage we did this, so that eventually I wasn't constantly lost, but gradually gained a clearer idea of where I was even in these huge fields empty of any conventional landmarks, since one hill looks much like another. As I learned the geography of the wilderness, Peter was teaching me about the animals and birds which inhabited it. Without direct teaching I was learning to read the sky for weather, the habits of range cattle by spending days with them, the precise composition of the shortgrass vegetation by crossing over it day after day. I began to observe the passages of the moon. Like most urban people, I had never even paid attention to the moon before coming to the country to live; I was so embarrassed that I didn't even tell Peter that I was paying attention nightly to her for the first time in my life. I knew nothing about the moon's phases, about her rhythms, about where she rose and where she set. As I gradually learned what to expect from her night after night, month after month, a kind of awe was dawning in me, and I was gaining a hint of what it was that made Peter so secure and calm.

I wanted to tell everyone about my discoveries — no, I wanted first to understand them clearly, then tell everyone. But these weren't things you could tell people, I was realizing. *Did you know the moon has phases?* My friends would have thought I'd lost my mind. And anyway, such a question hardly conveyed the magnitude or quality of my real discovery, which was closer to something like this: life makes sense, or the world has a governing body, or the power and beauty of Nature *is* astounding.

I wanted to tell everyone, but the people I now lived with already knew these things, whether they spoke of them or not, and I could not convey in conversation any of them to my old friends, if they'd been around to listen, which they weren't. As a way out of my frustration, I wrote them down. I did this with no clear reason in mind; I certainly wasn't thinking of turning them into a book or even of sending them to anyone else to read. I wrote them out of a deep drive, a need to fully assimilate them, so extraordinary did they seem at the time that I couldn't think of them as *my life* until I had in some familiar way concretized them.

In these early notes I tell, in utilitarian prose, exactly what happened. For example, there is a three-page record, dated February 9/78, of our adventure one evening going by snowmobile in the middle of a five-day blizzard to visit a neighbor a few miles away. (The snow had drifted across the road in fingers that were as deep as eight feet, sloping up on one side, and dropping abruptly off on the other. We had to drag the snowmobile up the sloping side, then Peter drove it down the cliffside, braking all the way so as not to go end for end. We did this for almost two miles before we reached a flat field that was smooth driving. It was worse going home at one in the morning, but anybody blizzard-bound for four days will tell you it was worth it.) Before that detailed description, I found a paragraph of ruminations about the rural value system.

By May 1979, exactly three years after my new life began, I was writing notes in a consistent pattern. I have kept journals continuously since, although their character changed fairly quickly from detailed, factual accounts of events to the psychic journey I was already, without knowing it, launched on.

I couldn't be with Peter all the time; I needed time to myself, and I had housework to do and cooking and clothes-washing. Sometimes Peter was out fencing with his hired man and didn't need me, or he was off at a cattle sale or a farm auction, or working with other men at one or the other grazing cooperatives. All of these meant that I was often alone in the house, working by myself.

In those first years I was trying to be a traditional country wife, and in the trying, I often felt that I was living in history. Both houses were very small and very old; although both had electricity and running water in the kitchen, neither had central heating systems or indoor bathrooms. I had been raised that way, it's true, but I'd had these conveniences all my adult life. Although most of the women I was meeting in the country not only had lived that very traditional life as children but also to some degree as adults, I was one of the few who still did, partly because once children were born, women's lives were more circumscribed — many of them gave up riding and working outdoors with their husbands except during seeding or harvest — and because then, after the pioneering period was over, efforts would be made to provide them with running water, indoor bathrooms and central heating. Many of my new acquaintances who were close to my age had had babies in diapers when they had no running water. But memories of that life, about which many of them were ambivalent, were very clear and familiar to all of them who'd been raised in the West.

I was, of course, suffering for this traditional life in all the ways traditional country wives suffered: physical exhaustion, the occasional sense of being out of fit with my own feminine nature, and my own peculiar nature as an individual human being, though I didn't really know what my own nature might turn out to be, and having occasional yearnings to dress up, paint my fingernails and curl my hair, and go somewhere elegant and luxurious and be waited on.

Of that period my journal says:

My right hand has a blackened fingernail from pumping water where I hit the pumpjack on the downward stroke. [Our water system had frozen underground and we were pumping water by hand into June when it finally thawed.] *My right thumb is sprained from helping load two-year-old steers. I was poking a big stick through the chute railings and the steer I was trying to move backed up, jamming my hand between my stick and the log railings. I thought my thumb was broken. I have a rope burn on the palm of my left hand. I was watering one of the horses and it jerked away from me, and tonight I cut my finger slicing vegetables.*

I was learning to be a different kind of woman from the one who'd danced all night in clubs to rock 'n' roll, competed with men at a job, borrowed money at the bank, bought a house, had a manicure, and set her cap for men and fended off others, who faced an urban, modern world on her own. As I lived this new way part of me was beginning to feel all that — the life of the modern, urban woman — had been a mistake, and maybe not the great improvement on my mother's life I thought it had been.

The ranch house had a cast-iron cookstove in the kitchen used more for heat now than for cooking, although Peter liked to make the breakfast coffee on it, swearing it tasted better, and a propane heater in the living room. The bedrooms were unheated. At the ranch in late fall when it might become as cold as minus fifty degrees Fahrenheit, even on seasonably cold days in the spring and fall, Peter and I had to keep the cookstove fired up to keep warm.

In a country where there were no trees and therefore no wood, people saved old fence posts and the wood from granaries or shacks that had been torn down to use as firewood. In the early days they'd burned buffalo chips till they were all gone from the prairie, then those who couldn't afford coal and had no wood collected and burned cow chips.

In the dirt cellar at the ranch there was still a little coal left, which on the coldest days I would add to the fire so it would burn longer. Then I remembered my youth in small-town Saskatchewan and the coal shuttle beside the kitchen cookstove and the shiny black pile in the basement under the coal chute where we would be sent to collect it.

But before I could add the fence posts Peter had first sawed into manageable lengths and then chopped into chunks that would fit into the stove, I had to collect chips of wood and long slivers with which to start the fire. Before long all the chips and slivers at the woodpile from Peter's last chopping session would be used up. Then I would put on my boots and jacket, scarf and mitts, and go out to range through all the corners of the yard to search, kicking aside snow or rooting in the tall grass, gathering small pieces of wood with which to start and keep my fire going. I would find myself falling into a reverie as I walked, sounds in the already silent yard muffled by the falling snow, the vistas blurred and narrowed by it, nobody around for miles, and I would have this sense of having moved into another world.

It was a world where things were what they seemed to be; where they were clear and simple and made a kind of sense so elemental that I didn't have to learn them and I didn't have to think at all with my mind. I thought instead with my bones and my muscles, with some deeply human place in my gut.

Then I would go in and build a fire and nurse it while I cooked on the propane stove and read or wrote, waiting until Peter returned. *Today is the sixth day that I have been alone here every day*, I wrote in my journal. It was my third spring of living that way.

I had to wear long underwear inside and out, partly because I had to go to an outdoor toilet, and though everything was old and worn out and even ugly by my own standards and life was stripped to the absolute basics and, with my college degrees obtained with such struggles so I wouldn't have to live like this, I was doing hard physical labor, I found myself moving in beauty. I found my life beautiful.

I was experiencing firsthand what I knew from their stories and from my earliest memories had been the lives of my mother, my aunts and my grandmothers. That was deeply gratifying, despite those very real physical

46

hardships, in a way I don't feel able to articulate other than to say that it had to do with some primal sense of womanhood stemming both from what I knew of their lives, and from an unconscious tribal memory, much more basic than mere family history, and which I had not even known existed.

It was also this: I was learning to live in Nature, shaping my life, my everyday activities in a direct way according to the weather, the seasons, the rising and setting of the sun and the moon. I was once again becoming aware of Nature's all-powerful presence. If anyone had asked me, I would still have been unable to say what might be learned from Peter asleep among his animals on the prairie as I had seen him that first summer, but I was learning it. I was learning it slowly, painfully, in solitude and silence and out of my own experience.

Every once in a while, with great relief — because I hadn't yet fully accepted my new life as permanent, or was satisfied that conditions would remain the way they so far had been — I would go *home*, back to the city to visit my family, and to see my son who was living with his father and his new wife in order to go to high school in the city. I would call up my dearest women friends and meet them for a drink when they'd finished their day's work.

As affectionate and empathic toward me as ever, they would question me about my new life. I would try to answer. I could speak in facts, but I couldn't go any further. Their questions, though, seemed never to be about facts, but instead were about my emotional life, my relationship with my new husband and my new community. I didn't know the answers to those questions, or if deep down I did know the answers, they hadn't yet floated up to the conscious level and I couldn't articulate them.

And, in the face of their questions, I felt powerless about my life, not just in concrete ways such as that I no longer had a job and therefore had no money of my own, or that I didn't own a car and lived so far from town that what hadn't mattered in the city now was a basic determinant of existence. I didn't know how to talk about this either because I hadn't come to terms with my new dependence, knowing that it wasn't unusual in traditional marriages, that I had voluntarily chosen it, that I wasn't convinced that my relationship with Peter had settled into what would be its final form, or that if I tried to explain I could make my friends, all feminists to some degree, understand. And if they did ask me about facts, neither was I always sure what the facts were.

I felt powerless too because, having moved into a community where I had no family and no friends, no one who would stand exclusively by me as an ally, I felt myself at the mercy of the family into which I had married and the community into which I had moved. I was not expecting to be, nor in any way prepared to be, fully self-sufficient. Those long, intimate conversations with my friends, founded as they were on a mutual lifestyle, which had once been the most important thing in my life aside from my child, were no longer relevant in terms of what I was going through. I, who had never been at a loss for words, had run out of things to say.

In fact, I was discovering the truth in the dictum "You can't go home again." I clung to my old world, terrified I was losing something valuable in myself by losing touch with it, but at the same time I had made a commitment to my new world and I was trying desperately to understand it and make a place for myself in it.

For a variety of reasons, I had not completed my thesis for my master's degree when Peter and I decided to marry. I had carried with me to the ranch boxes of papers: copies of research articles pertinent to it, the actual test papers of the many children who'd taken part in my study — about the validity and usefulness of a new children's intelligence test — the preliminary proposal, sheets of data from the computer and all the versions of the thesis itself of which I had had only one chapter left to write when I decided to give it up.

I had brought many books with me as well as household articles and personal belongings; there was simply no room for those boxes of now useless papers. I kept saying I would burn them, but as a measure of my difficulty in accepting that my old life, however ill-suited to me, was truly over, I made this entry in my journal:

I was burning my papers that I have kept around now for three years and not looked at. As I burned them I was very careful not to read anything. I thought, these papers are memories. If I don't look at them, I won't remember. So I am burning memories . . . But this thought led to whether I could burn all my papers instead of selected trivia. I debated and I . . . realized that I am the one who refuses to let the past go. It isn't people in the present . . . it is I who am afraid to let go because I have been afraid to make a final, permanent commitment to this place and this life.

For a long time I was to hover partly in each, without solid footing in either one.

I had so much to learn before I could call this place home. Listening to neighbors in conversation, listening to Peter, watching the countryside and asking questions, I began to build a fund of facts which would contribute to my eventually feeling at home. When I first arrived here I knew nothing of the history of the area or its people or of the land, although Peter — at his best in talking about the land itself — soon taught me that the soil quality was poor, mostly brown soils, pale and sickly looking to someone who'd been raised on the rich black loam of the fertile central part of the province, and that it was a region of such meager precipitation as to be officially classified as semiarid, a heartbreaking one step up from desert.

The first farmers had arrived only about seventy-five years before, and they had faced such hardship that during the twenties and the Depression the government had actually to move whole families out to better land or it was feared they would starve to death. In districts with good soil and adequate rains it was possible to arrive from Europe with nothing and after a few years of farming to be comfortably off. This was never true in the southwest, Peter told me. We were now living among second- and sometimes third-generation farmers and only rarely, when people had been lucky enough to settle in good pockets, had any of them had any real prosperity.

Abruptly, just after I arrived, all this changed. It began to rain, wheat prices soared — durum went to an all-time high of over eight dollars a bushel — and the Wheat Board was able to find markets for all of it. Farmers, our neighbors, suddenly had money, some of them a lot of it, and for the first time farm families were able to enjoy some of the amenities of life that urban people had been taking for granted for years.

The first money went to buy the latest farming equipment: air seeders replaced drills, combines got so big that the biggest of them could fill a three-ton grain truck in about two minutes, and four-wheel-drive tractors as big as small houses appeared overnight in farmers' fields. Although our grain gave a nice bonus to our income too, Peter held firm to his decision when he'd first taken over the place in the mid-sixties: he was not a farmer, he didn't like farming, he was now too old to spend the almost quarter of a million dollars it would take to buy a full set of the best farming equipment. All around us the shortgrass prairie was being plowed up to grow more wheat — the government was encouraging farmers in this by subsidizing new breaking — and as it disappeared Peter was filled with regret. He would never allow a plow to touch his if he could help it, he said.

Such is the fragility of this landscape that even today a practised eye can spot land that was broken as long as seventy or more years ago and then allowed to go back to Nature; nobody knows if it will ever return to its original condition. Peter's school pony trail from the ranch house over hill and dale the four and a half miles down to his old school at what is now the nonexistent town of Divide is still easy to see. The school pony trail almost a mile away made by a man who died in old age remains an eroding scar on the landscape I can see from my front window when the light strikes it the right way.

We did, in the third year of our marriage, build a new house, though; God knows, we needed it if anybody did. All around us new houses were at last springing up, since most people were still living in the houses their parents had built in the forties and fifties which were far too small, and hopelessly worn out so that they let in flies and cold air and rain and, worst of all, were riddled with mice. I wanted to build it at the ranch. I thought it would be paradise to live all day, every day, in the midst of such beauty. The remoteness seemed to me a bonus.

But Peter wouldn't hear of it. "You've never wintered here," he told me — although I'd lived there into January two years running. "In the winter the wind never stops blowing and there's no shelter, the roads are always drifted in so you can't get out, and it's too far to the nearest neighbor, never mind the nearest town." He was adamant, and I had by this time learned that in such matters, given his experience, he was always right. We built our new house on the hay farm in the valley, and although I have learned to love this place as much as the ranch, I still have days when I regret not living there.

The new prosperity allowed people to travel, too. For a few years there in the late seventies and early eighties the winter trip to Hawaii or Mexico was de rigueur among farm families. Even Peter and I had two short holidays in Mexico during those years, paid for by wheat, not by cattle. Whole gangs of neighbors and their families went into Montana to ski each winter, too, but the ultimate must have been the winter some ten couples, all friends and neighbors — not including Peter and myself — booked a separate tour and went together on a two-week trip to Mexico.

I couldn't help but look with some envy at our neighbors, but Peter kept telling me that the new prosperity of the farmers was just a boom before the inevitable bust, that Palliser had been right: this was dry country and would be dry again, and no matter what the crop scientists were doing and saying, you still needed rain to grow wheat. He also said that soil fertility in the area, never great to begin with, was rapidly being depleted by the new farming practices — huge, heavy machinery, chemical fertilizers, monocropping, repeated summerfallowing — and that eventually a price would be exacted by the land for their use.

It is a strange thing to live in the midst of a culture changing so abruptly. Although I was taking some part in all of this — the new house, the trips to Mexico — I felt to some degree removed from it, partly because we weren't really farmers and our income was only slightly different from what it had always been, and because I viewed everything that happened in my new community from the vantage point of somebody who was slowly and painfully learning she would never be anything but an outsider.

And I was still reveling in the freedom of my new life despite the inevitable loneliness, and in the real balm for the heart and soul of waking each morning to birdsong and the open sky, and going to bed each night listening to the muted croak of the nighthawk and the distant, melodious choir of coyote voices. Submerged in the truly wondrous present, and surrounded by a community of which most of the members in their newfound prosperity seemed to have no worries, I didn't think much about the future, either for myself or for them.

Instead, I found solace in the extraordinary beauty of the land itself. On a warm spring day riding a horse, walking or traveling in a truck across true shortgrass prairie that had never known a plow in all its history since the glaciers, I thought I had never smelled anything so wonderful in my life: sage and grasses mixed with sunlight, carried on the light fresh air as it swept freely across miles of unbroken grass.

Peter taught me to see the grassland through his eyes and to love it as he did. If native grassland was disappearing from the farms all around us, Peter hung on even more fiercely to all he had control of that had never been broken since the soil was deposited by the glaciers in the previous geological era. I had, and still have, all the prairie wilderness I need to look at and walk on and, as the years of my new life here have passed, that land has become more important to me than I would ever have thought possible.

Because I was alone a great deal, still had no close friends to visit and not much housework, and I could only read or write so much, walking had long since become part of my daily routine. I walked every day, I told people, to keep fit; in my heart I knew I was using walking as a reason to be outdoors since, aside from my small and usually unsuccessful garden (with the short growing season, the fierce summer heat, the constant, killing wind and the poor soil, I was having to learn to garden all over again), and my occasional days spent out riding with Peter, I had no other practical reason to spend an hour or two in Nature each day.

Walking was a way to pass the time, to familiarize myself at a deep level with my new environment, to enjoy what was fast becoming to me the best thing in my new life — the landscape. It didn't require a member-ship, social skills or specialized skills, companions, a vehicle, money, a weapon, or even a special costume. All I had to do was open the door, pick a direction and start walking. I had to be careful to avoid fields I knew had bulls in them, or in the spring especially, cows with new calves, but on such a big place this was easy to do.

As time passed and I grew familiar with the landscape and the small land-marks on it, my walks grew less aimless. When I left the house, I usually had a destination in mind: a rock, a spot on the riverbank, a particular coulee, or just a stretch of country road that was especially isolated where I almost never encountered a vehicle. I became familiar with each field within walk-ing distance of either house. Some fields I liked better than others to walk in because the view was better, or I always saw antelope there, or it seemed to me I felt better there. Each field had its own character.

There is a place in one of the fields at the ranch, though, which I always hated riding in because whenever we were there I could feel my horse tens-ing, changing his steady gait to an uneven prance and throwing his head, resisting my direction. I could feel him wanting to break into a gallop, or to rear and, expecting at any second to be bucked off or to fall as he bolted, I tightened my legs and shortened the reins, and talked to him, as Peter had taught me to do.

The only reason I could think of for this strange behavior was the way the wind swept down through a break in the hills right there, reaching us across twenty miles of uninhabited grassland, and I thought he must catch its scent of wilderness and freedom coming through that long draw down the fields. Once past that stretch of land, he would settle down. Although that field always affected my horse, it affected me not at all, and I've never bothered going there to walk.

But the field that seemed different to me is a quarter section of native grassland with the nearest human dwelling only a mile away. I remember walking there once during the first summer I spent here and I continued to go there, although not very often since it's some distance from the house, because it is so much more pleasant to walk in wilderness than down a country road. And for a long time — years — I tended to hold that field in reserve for the days when it felt right to go there, not that I could explain what that means, other than that, I see now, it had a different and puzzling feel to it, which caused me to approach it in a less offhand way.

Since the Butalas had bought it, it had rarely been grazed by cattle and, since it was too steep and stony to break for farming, it has remained very much the way it had been since the melting of the last glaciers. In time, going there became a special pleasure because of that exhilarating, gritty *feel* to the air there, and because I had learned to find in a landscape which most might find chillingly sparse and uneventful, a unique beauty. I attributed my desire to be there to the taint of wildness I could feel, although why I should have felt it there more than in any of the other fields I walked in I didn't know. But of all the land Peter owned, it became my favorite place to walk.

Occasionally, during the first year, I would take a book with me, intending to sit on the grass far from any signs of the presence of humans, and read. I did this because I thought I might otherwise be bored, I suppose, because of all those years at the university where I was never without a book. I found, and this greatly surprised me, that reading was boring in the middle of such splendor — splendor that saturated all the senses, not merely the vision — that reading was clearly meaningless in this context. I needed only the prairie, I discovered, whether I saw wildlife or not, whether a flower bloomed in a ten-mile radius or not. Just the ground, the feel of it underfoot, the thin cover of club moss and wild grasses, the stones, these were enough — more than enough.

In that particular stony field I learned much that I had not dreamt of before it began to teach me; I had experiences there that changed my life. In time these strange things that began to happen to me when I was out on the prairie, not only in that particular field, but in others as well, began to come together for me to gradually form a shadowy but increasingly powerful whole. I was discovering something about living in Nature that I had never heard anyone speak of, or read in any books, though it might have been in some of them if I'd had the eyes to read it there.

Many of my writer friends who love to spend time in Nature have their own numinous experiences to tell me of as we walk together or lie on the grass watching the sky: communicating with wild animals, seeing things which aren't there in the everyday sense, learning things from people who are not present, being flooded with new understanding. I begin, despite official silence on the subject by much of religion and most scientists, to think such experiences are so widespread and frequent as to be the norm rather than the unusual. It seems inarguable to me that, as Erich Neumann wrote in "Mystical Man," "Man is by nature a *homo mysticus.*"

I have said, "This is the place where words stop," referring to that moment when, out in Nature, not shooting, collecting, studying, naming or farming, we realize that an entity is present, or that Nature is alive, even that Nature has a memory. I meant by this that suddenly there seem to be no words to describe adequately our experiences, no familiar phrases or colloquialisms to fall back on, no single nouns or verbs which have been given over to the sole purpose of describing such awareness.

I think we have so allowed the scientific approach to the world to take over our perceptions that we are afraid to mention such experiences for fear of being laughed at or vilified. When we do, we find ourselves stammering, struggling for words, never being able to convey in language to our own satisfaction exactly what it felt like or looked like or what sensations it evoked in us. We struggle against skepticism, our own as much as anyone else's, and in time we lapse into silence about them and a whole, valuable dimension of human experience remains unsung and unvalidated.

It is hard not to be very angry with scientists for this loss. Their unshakable belief in a materialistic, purely objective world has so permeated our culture that only in religious life are we allowed the slightest latitude in the dimensions of what we might call the "real." Scientists have specialized in narrowing experience, told us that the only truths possible are the ones they know; they have developed specialized languages the rest of us don't understand and have elevated themselves, and been elevated by us, to the status of those who *know*, while poets, visionaries and mystics have been relegated to the realm of the crazy.

We use words like "awareness," "perception," "sense," or "intuition," or a "sixth sense." They are as close as our language, as far as I know, allows us to come to describe the way in which we apprehend experience that is out of the realm of the ordinary. None of these words seem quite sufficient. And as for describing the quality of the experience, its texture, color and the accompanying emotion, the way it permeates our being and floods us with new knowledge/awareness/perception, it seems to be impossible to find the right words and a way to structure them that will make our listeners believe us.

Until one has had an experience of this sort, one cannot *hear* what one who has had these experiences is saying. Those of us who allow these experiences room in our psyches, who do not refuse or deny them, know we are walking a narrow ledge with psychosis on one side and scientism on the other. It is a dangerous journey we gladly make, putting one foot carefully before the other, our arms out to maintain our balance, our concentration on the path absolute. The world is more wonderful than any of us have dared to guess, as all great poets have been telling us since the invention of poetry. To discover these truths we don't need to scale Mount Everest or white-water raft the Colorado or take up skydiving. We need only go for walks.

I had been here five long years when I dreamt this dream: it was night, but so clear and bright it was almost as light out as during the day. I was standing inside the door of the back porch of the old ranch house. In the dream the door was divided in the center into an upper and a lower part which opened separately. I was looking out the open top half at the sky watching in awe and wonder a gigantic eagle as it soared over the ranch. It was so big that with its wings outspread it covered the entire yard, which is about twenty fenced acres. It had a slender, stylized body and wings and it was a smooth, delicate pale gray. Its beauty was entrancing. Even now, remembering it, something in my viscera opens into an infinitude that frightens me.

In front of me, on the rectangle of cement at the door, stood an owl which was at least six feet tall. It was also a creature of stunning beauty, a pale brown with deep turquoise fan-shaped regularly spaced markings on its breast. The eagle soared above us and as I watched it, the owl watched me and repeatedly bumped its body against the door in front of me, which was not latched, as if it was trying to get into the porch with me. It wasn't threatening and I wasn't afraid. I simply glanced at it and kept it out while I watched the eagle.

I puzzled over the meaning of the dream. All I knew was that it was far too wonderful to be ignored or dismissed. I knew as well as I'd ever known anything that, although I had no idea how I would do it, I would have to find out what it meant. So beautiful, so mystical a dream must have something to do with the new life I was leading, but I did not know exactly what. I didn't consciously know then how profoundly my move out of the urban, academic, feminist world into the country and rural life had shaken me. My very atoms would be rearranged. In time it would be a surprise to look in the mirror and see the same, if aging, face staring back at me, when the person inside felt utterly different.

ANOMIE

My first year or two here as I began to settle in, during the time when I was still following Peter on his daily round of work and driving in the truck with him from ranch to hay farm and back again, I would awake in the morning, try to recall what we'd done the day before, and draw a complete blank. I would put my mind to it, giving myself clues: had we ridden horses? Had we been to town, any town? Had we visited neighbors? Nothing. It bewildered and frightened me to be completely unable to remember one thing about the previous day.

Then I would ask Peter; he would think for a minute before saying, "We loaded the cancer-eye cow and took her to the vet," or, "We went riding," or, "We fixed that cattle oiler." Sometimes it took a second question about where the cattle oiler had been, or the cancer-eye cow, before the day would come back to me. It was always a relief when I remembered something, no matter how small or how vaguely.

I struggled to understand. With my academic background in aspects of human behavior, I thought I ought to be able to understand the significance of my inability to remember. But at the same time as I tried with various arguments to reassure myself that nothing serious was happening to my brain, I was undeniably frightened, especially on the days when nothing I suggested to myself would bring back one memory, not clear, not fuzzy, of the previous day. All I could come up with as an explanation was that for the previous four and more years I had been living in such a state of tension, under so much pressure day by day in my work and in my private life, that now, with the pressure off for the first time since I'd grown up, something inside me had let go, had left its post, had sat down on the job.

Besides this inexplicable forgetfulness, I felt guilty. It would be ten o'clock in the morning and I'd be wearing jeans, boots and a down-filled riding jacket, sitting in the truck beside Peter, daydreaming. I'd snap to attention thinking, I should be at work! before I'd remember that I didn't have a job anymore, that for the first time since I was sixteen and had gotten my first job, I didn't have to be anywhere and wasn't about to get into trouble for not doing whatever I was supposed to be doing. Remembering that fact brought only relief, but an element of the guilt always remained because my sisters and women friends were still slogging away, going to a job every day, as was most of the world, while I was so fortunate that I no longer had to. Habit was so strong that it took a full year before that sense of guilt that lay behind everything I did slowly dissolved.

By then I was working part-time as a resource person in Special Education and I began to spend less time with Peter as he went about his daily round. I understood enough about his world now, I was no longer baffled by what it was he did all day, and I had learned that there were some things I liked to be a part of and some I didn't. The sweetness of always being together was wearing off; we were becoming an old married couple. Although most of the time I still was, neither of us any longer took it for granted that I would always be with him during the day.

Peter was forty-one when we married; he had not been married before, and he had led the life of the country bachelor for a long time. If I was going through a hard time adapting to my new marriage and lifestyle, Peter needed a few years to get used to the condition of being married, which meant thinking and living as a team. While his bachelorhood had made him wonderfully independent when it came to getting himself something to eat, buying groceries, generally looking after himself, for a long time after we were married he kept on thinking like a bachelor, so that I often felt like a guest, a welcome one, but a guest nevertheless, instead of a partner as other rural wives are.

If, on the one hand, I had little envy of the women who had moved from their father's ranch or farm to the place they started with their husbands upon their marriage, missing the independence I'd known, on the other, I did envy them, because even if their names weren't on the actual deed, they could feel the farm or ranch was as much theirs as their husbands', because they had been there from the beginning. The place I lived on had been unbroken prairie when the Butalas first saw it; it had been in the Butala family for two generations. The world I'd stepped into I didn't even understand, could help with very little, much less imagine running on my own. I could never feel myself an equal partner with my husband in the enterprise, and all of that contributed to my sense of being alien and, increasingly as the years passed, apologetic, because where I'd once been a valued member of my own small society, in this new life, I was slowly assimilating a sense of my own uselessness.

And, of course, I hadn't reckoned with another fact of rural life, which is that the daughter-in-law has to earn her way into the family into which she's married, that other members of rural families are frequently grudging in their acceptance of her. This is, I think, usually at base a kind of xenophobia, difficulty in accepting a stranger into the midst of such close-knit families, a situation documented in cultures around the world. In some cases it seems to be tied to landownership, and the belief that a daughter-in-law is an intruder who has acquired property that without her would belong to the other family members, and the accompanying resentment because she has done nothing to earn it.

Peter's friends were men; most of our visitors were men; day in and day out I was surrounded by men. Nearly all the daily conversation I listened to was man-talk: machinery, land, animals, farm economics. If on the one hand I was overwhelmed by the vast array of knowledge about the world men who led a life in agriculture had, on the other, I was frequently bored stiff and often resentful that I had been reduced to pouring coffee and cooking meals for them. Occasionally I told them jokingly that they were desperately boring; they just laughed with that easy and careless grace of the male landowner secure in his unchallenged supremacy in his world.

The women included me in their activities, helped me when I asked for help: one of them taught me to can peaches, others taught me better ways to sew; they gave me badly needed gardening advice; when Peter wasn't around and they were talking about things having to do with farming and cattle that I didn't understand, they explained. At dances and suppers when Peter was off with the other men, they came and sat beside me and talked to me so I wouldn't feel alone. They invited me for coffee and they came to help, as they always had, when we were branding or rounding up or chasing cows. On the whole, I found them warm and kind. It was not their fault that this huge gap existed between us.

By the time I had been here a couple of years I was more at ease with the women. That is, I was friendly with five or six women to the extent that I was glad to see them, happy to go to their houses for coffee or an evening of talk, that I felt comfortable with them and empathic toward the tribulations and pleasures of their lives. Together we had found a level where we got on very well, could carry on conversations, share jokes, enjoy each other's company. Today I think of three or four of those women as my friends, maintaining a distinction between acquaintances and friends, and I believe if asked, they would say the same of me. But I don't see any of them every day; sometimes I don't see them for weeks, or even months. One of my first lessons about the nature of friendship in the country is that the deepest friendships take years — even a lifetime — to build, that there is no sense of urgency about it, as it seemed to me there is in the city, where it seemed essential to speak with close friends three or four times a week and to do things together at least once a week, if not more often, month after month, year after year, where any great hiatus in companionship meant the friendship was largely over.

I was beginning to see that one profound effect of viewing the world always from the same vantage point is to endow one with a sense of timelessness; that is, with a sense of there being time for everything, and also of a sense of the rhythmic nature of time: the cycle of the seasons, of the sun and the moon, which spills over also into the understanding of human life as cyclical. One is born, goes through infancy, childhood, adolescence, adulthood, maturity, old age. One dies at the same time as others are born, and so on. And this steady cycle of human life is very clear and immediate in rural life where people attending a neighbor's wedding might remember helping get the bride's mother to the hospital the day the bride was born, and at a funeral might remember an illness of the deceased fifty years before, and how it was similar to an ailment of his grandfather's.

Urban life confuses this elemental knowledge, disturbs it in many ways, for example, by separating children from adults in most social situations, and retired people from working people, and by allowing the culture of the teenager — which is not to say that this latter doesn't happen in the country, too, but out here children are raised as workers in the family enterprise, and as a result of this, boys gain a sense of manhood and girls of womanhood very early, so that teenagerhood is neither so pronounced nor so different. All of this, it seems to me, nourishes in one a firm and very basic sense of stability and security — sad to say, now being disturbed by the agricultural crisis — and a sense that everything will come round again in due course without there being any need to push it.

But, oh, I longed to talk! I yearned with a desire that was close to heartbreak to sit down close to a good woman friend and say to her in an undertone, "It's like this, you see? And this and this and this. I feel — it seems to me — I can't make sense of —" And I imagined her sobriety, the depth in her eyes as she listened, the serious, gentle warmth as she replied. How good I would feel after, with how much more strength I would be able to face my new life.

Sometimes when I asked questions of one of the women I was meeting, I felt a misunderstanding between myself and her. I could see in her face and the way she moved her hands that she was defensive about her life, thinking I was scornful or that I knew things I didn't know or wanted to know things that were apparently common knowledge in the community, but about which I hadn't even an inkling at the time, and if I had I would never have dreamt of asking about. I wanted to know what I had asked, that was all; my new acquaintances did not understand the depth of my ignorance, nor the depth of my longing to *feel* how their lives were, so that I might find a way to belong.

Now when I ran into the inevitable small cruelties of society, they hurt me out of all proportion to their significance, because here I was powerless, had no one to turn to — for what did Peter know of women's ways? — and I was without family or friends to defend me. With a touch of paranoia, I began to feel that people were trying to cut me down to size, to abrade me into the same shape and form that they had themselves. Filled with frustration and anger I wrote in my journal: *They try to make you forget who you are.*

One day in the second year of our marriage, it occurred to me that I might write a novel. The notion simply popped into my head and I immediately dismissed it as a ridiculous idea, not to mention embarrassingly clichéd. But I kept thinking about it, and finally, telling myself that if it turned out I couldn't do it nobody needed to know, that nobody needed ever to see one word I wrote, in great excitement, I actually began a novel.

It was set in the city and its protagonist was a woman, a single parent, a person with a career and all those urban concerns that had until so recently been mine. Even while I was working on it I knew my subject matter had already been done to death by a thousand published writers. But, failing to consider the possibilities with any seriousness, I thought I had nothing else to write about.

As I wrote I began to realize that even though I had read more novels than I could count, I had never paid any attention to how writers put novels together, and I discovered that a novelist couldn't possibly tell the whole story, that the reader filled in many gaps in some way I wasn't sure of, but thought had to be given clues by the writer. But I wasn't sure what those clues might be, and I wasn't sure that what I had written so far had given the clues which would lend the work a coherent narrative flow. I began to feel confused and uncertain about what to do next, and before long, in some perplexity, I had given up.

Somewhere I think I still have those fifty or so pages. When I lost the thread of that novel, the exhilaration of it, I thought of short stories. Surely, I thought to myself, it must be easier to write short stories. I mentioned my interest to somebody on the district Community College Committee, and next thing I knew I was driving into Eastend to attend an evening class on the writing of short stories. Our doctor at that time was British and his wife, our teacher, was an Oxford graduate with a degree in English Literature, a brilliant woman with a bottomless fund of knowledge, and as I later discovered, a talented writer herself. That short-lived class — four or five evenings, I think — launched me as a writer.

Well, it wasn't easier to write short stories. Yet, all the while I struggled with them, writing and revising and writing them again and again, I held in my mind the novel I would one day write.

I was by then thirty-eight years old and I had finally discovered that I had wanted to be a writer since I was nine years old and had indeed written a novel. This was a childhood memory I'd suppressed, or simply forgotten, which came back to me while I was attending that night class. It is probably more accurate to say only that as a child I had tried to write a book, that I had been so excited by the idea when I thought of it that the wonderful feeling it produced inside me was akin to the day — the year before when I'd made my First Communion — when a cloud came down and lit inside my chest. I didn't then conceive of the notion of being a writer; I don't believe I'd ever conceived before even of the notion that somebody had written the books I borrowed from the library and that we used in school — certainly no teacher had ever pointed this out.

My mother, who was an almost obsessive reader and who insisted my sisters and I read all the great books of her own childhood, from the Oz series to the L.M. Montgomery books to Dickens, had probably mentioned authors in passing, but I doubt directly connecting them to the words on the page, and I had failed to make the connection myself. In this milieu, my idea of writing a book myself had to have been a purely creative act, and the wonderful feeling the idea elicited, in retrospect, an object lesson, both for how my life should have been guided from that time on and for the value of encouraging all children in creative acts.

My first novel had been about eight pages long, and when I showed it to my mother she'd been very excited and pleased, too, and had helped me make a construction paper cover for it and had found a length of bright red wool in her knitting basket with which we tied it together. I will always be grateful to her for her help and especially for her enthusiasm, which even as a child I could see was genuine. I am sorry to say that my little book was lost years ago. I even have a vague but not too trustworthy memory of throwing it away myself in disappointment and frustration because what I had thought was so wonderful, magical almost, and laden with meaning meant nothing to anyone else but my mother, and neither of us knew exactly what it meant or what to do about it.

The day as an adult I thought of writing a novel was hardly different emotionally from that day in great excitement as a child I had first made that decision. Now, thirty years later, I was beginning to believe that the person inside me had always been a writer, more specifically a novelist, that I would never consider myself a writer until I had written a novel.

Although I grew more serious about it with every piece I wrote, for the time being writing was still a hobby. My stories were about the agricultural people and agricultural life around me. I wasn't yet using writing as an instrument of self-knowledge, although I had already begun that first, surprising probing into what really makes the world go round: people's motivations, their secret, even unconscious desires, what they must surely love or hate, revealed not by what they declared but teased out from the way they moved their bodies, or blinked or looked away, by their actions, or by small, half-heard asides.

At the same time as, with such delight and wonder, I was taking my first tottering steps as a writer, it is surprising to look back on the record in my journals of my loneliness and unhappiness. That is, as fascinating as writing was from the very beginning, and as fulfilling as it came to be, it was no magic elixir to cure whatever seemed to be ailing me. My dramatic change in lifestyle, compounded by the joint decision to allow my son Sean to go to high school in the city, had precipitated a profound personal and spiritual crisis. The record in my journals of this psychic struggle, mixed with my learning to be a writer, is confused and convoluted, its many parts so intertwined that they can't be extricated and set in a neat row: first this, then this, then this.

I had set out on one life as a young woman of twenty-one; I had struggled down that path for fourteen years when suddenly I had come to a gaping hole, an impassable, black abyss into which the path had broken off and disappeared. I looked back, but the path I had walked on for so long was now filled with cracks and obstacles and places where it was obliterated. I could not go back; I could not go forward. I had closed my eyes and leaped, and when I opened them again I found myself in another country where I didn't speak the language or know the customs, where I was an outsider, an intruder, an alien, where I was alone.

I became more and more meditative, examining encounters over and over again from every direction, sometimes blaming others, sometimes blaming myself for what seemed clear to me was my failure to fit in. I questioned my own motivations and my behavior and my true desires. Was I argumentative? Was I unkind? Was I difficult? Was I peculiar? Yes, I answered to all four, and a lot more besides. But if I was self-critical, bewildered, saddened, sometimes belligerent, the more profound effect on me was to make me write in my journal in the spring of 1980, four years after my arrival, *I feel invisible here and dead.* At the very moment I was sensing my artistic power, I was facing a spiritual crisis of profound proportions.

Peter never changed. I often thought how well named he was, a rock, and how fortunate I was to have his calm, stability and strength beside me during such a time. He went about his daily round of work year after year, altering the pattern of it if he grew bored, keeping an eye on the markets and on the weather and on the flow of events in the world of agriculture, considering himself to be one of the blessed in that he had his place in which to live out his life doing what he loved. He went about his business and I went about mine, and we took comfort in each other's presence. Every morning he got up and went out to work in the fields cutting and baling and hauling hay, chasing cows or rounding them up, doctoring or feeding them, calving, branding, weaning. He was often gone from first light to last. I never told him of the anguish I was going through. I never told anyone.

But not only was my new life starting to change the way I felt, it was starting to change the way I perceived the world. Sitting on horseback I would watch the thousand-pound, horned range cows as they plodded past me with their calves on the way to water and I would be thinking about the sheer mystery of them, studying them to feel their consciousness, what it was they saw and smelled and knew. Once I asked, a little tentatively, "They really aren't very smart, are they?" and Peter replied after a moment, sounding a bit surprised, but too polite to simply disagree and having his own problems with articulating what he knew, "They know what they need to know." "Smart," as I was using the word, I came to understand in time, was simply a wrong-headed way to think about animals.

Living in the midst of distance, in a world where distance was an entity and not a mere dimension, the vast, omnipresent sky beginning to feel more like a creature than mere space, although I wasn't consciously aware of it, were all working away inside me, beginning to enact profound changes in my city-dweller's psyche. If I merely felt twinges of something beyond awe and pleasure in the beauty around me, I didn't ponder what those twinges were, or even clearly conceptualize them.

I had begun to dream my strange, powerful, beautiful dreams more frequently. I would awake in the morning and recall them clearly and in every detail. They stunned me and filled me with awe. I knew I could not simply forget them; I felt certain that each one meant something and that it was imperative to find out what it was. Perhaps they held the key to my growing despair.

Immediately after the owl-eagle dream I bought a simple dream book, but its entries seemed silly and quixotic. I didn't know what it was I was looking for, but I knew this wasn't it. I grabbed at clues wherever I found them; in my reading I followed up references that looked pertinent, and from the references I followed further ones. I haunted bookstores when I was in the city, searching the shelves, I did not know precisely for what. As I grew more and more compulsive about this, certain books began to seem to jump off the shelf at me, books I hadn't heard of and knew nothing about. If, on a crowded shelf, I saw a book grow bright and separate before my eyes, I bought it, took it home and read it with total absorption.

I have no explanation for the way in which certain books which I knew nothing about, in a way rather like magical objects in fairy tales, or the cakes that in *Alice in Wonderland* bore labels that said "Eat me" would call my attention to them. I felt I was being helped in my quest for Self; I didn't try to discover by whom. If nothing else, I'd been raised to believe in guardian angels; it didn't, therefore, seem impossible to me that one who was truly, honestly searching might find help.

One of these books was Robert Monroe's *Journeys Out of the Body*, which I was embarrassed to be seen buying and read with skepticism. In a different class was Ernest Becker's Pulitzer Prize–winning *The Denial of Death*, which I had never heard of till the day in a bookstore when it seemed to order me to buy it. I regard it now as one of the most important books I've read because it clarified and put into perspective a nebulous world of ideas about the nature of humanity I had never even attempted to articulate in my life, much less strung together into a coherent whole, but which now had become the issues I was grappling with.

One day early on in this quest, in the university bookstore in Saskatoon, I came across three massive hardcover books in a sale bin: *The Oxford Classical Dictionary*, *The Golden Bough*, and a peculiar work called *Dictionary of All Scriptures and Myths*. I could hardly believe my eyes. I would never have been able to afford them if they hadn't been on sale, and that they were at that moment in my life seemed no accident at all but something akin to divine intervention. I bought all three and carried them home as if they were a king's treasure. I keep remembering — I think it's a Sufi belief — the saying that when the pupil is ready, the teacher will come. My teacher was to be books.

I devoured them: from Jung to Joseph Campbell to the Bible and *Bullfinch's Mythology*, from William James and Evelyn Underhill to Thomas Merton. My experiences out on the prairie with their mystical nature and my dream-life, together with my ruminations coming out of all that reading, were working to take me into books about mysticism itself. Then, in what seemed to me a natural progression, I began to read about Buddhism, Sufism, Taoism.

I could hardly believe I'd spent nine years on a university campus without ever dipping into any of these thinkers, could hardly believe I had thought myself educated, or that I knew anything at all about the world. I went about my household tasks, went riding with Peter, socialized with the neighbors, went for long daily walks, while all the while in outer silence, a whole new intellectual life was blooming inside me. With no one to talk about these things, appalled in any case at the very thought of telling anyone of the tremendous, life-threatening journey on which I had been launched, I turned to my journals to record my journey.

I didn't see it clearly at the time, but I was undergoing psychoanalysis, with myself as therapist to my own soul, for reading Jung to the extent I did and with such intensity I couldn't help but examine my own history, the story of my own life, which I began to mentally write, and sometimes put in my journal, for the first time. I began to comprehend that until I understood my own life I would not understand anything at all, and that

I could not go on trying to found a new life for myself, trying to make myself into a new person, till I had some clarity about my old life.

While I had never thought of my childhood as idyllic, my conscious memories had been of being a family, of the constant, if sometimes reluctant, companionship of my four sisters, of aunts and uncles and cousins by the dozen, of family picnics, Christmas gatherings, summer holidays, evenings at home reading books and listening to the radio, and in later years watching television. Now I began to ponder about the parts that I had always dismissed as unimportant incidents in a field of family warmth and closeness.

I began to examine my assumptions about myself, my place in my family, how my family had acted on me to make me into whatever it was I had become. I dredged up significant events I'd completely forgotten or had buried because they were too painful to think about. I began to understand, as a trivial example, the reasons why certain people in my childhood had been especially kind to me, something I'd always been grateful for, but had never considered before as needing an explanation. I examined over and over again my never very satisfactory relationship with my mother. I set myself exercises: what is the earliest thing I can remember?

I remembered, in answer to this, being in the northern part of the province where I'd been raised, on a gloomy, windy, cold day, either spring or fall. The memory begins with an adult who had been carrying me, setting me down to play in the roots of an old willow tree. I was bundled up in warm clothing and I had toys beside me. Across the way from me my older sister sat in the roots of another willow with her toys. I recall the scene from inside that two- or three-year-old's psyche: everything grayed and colorless, myself crying hard and loud, but most of all I remember how the world seemed utterly without hope or joy or love. I feel only absolute hopelessness; it is not coherent enough to call despair, but it is totally encompassing.

The next earliest childhood memory is much the same: I'm not crying, but the room in which I stand with my father and mother and sister seems so cold, not physically but emotionally, that the scene might be carved out of ice.

I have no idea what was happening in either scene and there is no one I can ask. In any case, there are no clues to place either event in the family history. They belong to an emotional history only, and to nobody else's but my own. I record them only to illustrate what I began to believe is an emotional bent I have toward despair; that is, that in my psyche the possiblity for despair, having been there from my infancy, is always closest to the surface, I suspect more so than in most people. Now, deeply, irreparably wounded by the breakdown of my first, fourteen-year marriage, I didn't need many bad experiences in my new life to bring it back to the surface.

I had begun to search my own soul for some grounding, some *thing* that was *me*, truly me, so that I might build on it and make myself into a person again. I began to see that I had never been my Self in the first place, that I had spent my life being what others had wanted me to be and as a result, never having rebelled, never having said *no* to anybody, I had no Self, or the self I was using, not being the true one, was thoroughly unstable, easily shaken, even destroyed. I was thrashing about in the ways I knew — reading, writing stories, thinking while out walking on the prairie by myself — for clues as to how one did this monumental work of self-creation.

I kept reading, searching for a point of view about life and ideas about a way to live that would be an anchor to cling to, or a beacon to guide me. I read St. John of the Cross — he of the dark night of the soul — till, appalled and angered, I threw him across the room. His ideas were fine if you were a monk — and who would be ill-advised enough to want to be a monk? — but I was daughter, sister, wife and mother. My world was grounded in my body; to deny my body, as he said, was tantamount to dying, and while that might make sense to men, it emphatically made none to me — worse, seemed downright sinful — for what had God given us this earthly life and such infinite beauty in which to live if he did not want us to use it and to enjoy it? The Christian mystics, the women, seemed utterly deluded to me; the sexuality of the language in which they wrote about their love of God embarrassed me.

Eventually, too, I became exasperated with the Zen Buddhists. I found them in love with their own rhetoric and their silly stories; the very complexity with which they chose to present what turned out to be simple ideas struck me as typically male; their humility seemed filled with male arrogance. The more I read them, the more I felt they were out of touch with the simple needs of the female being, a common person such as the world is filled with, trying to find a way to live her life within the given social structures and among other ordinary people.

I had come into this new life in the country and then into this period of mental anguish armed with only one dictum. I clung to it as well as I could; it was that no one would ever again tell me what I thought. If I was tumbling and tossing in a sea of misunderstanding and bad ideas, I was finally, in my forties, determined that they would be, at the very least, my own. I would never again accept anybody's word about anything having to do with my life unless, having examined it from every angle, matched it against how it felt in my heart, my gut, my head, I knew it fit my own real feelings, how I viewed life and my own real experiences. I, and nobody else, would determine what my own real experiences were and had been. I might be wrong, but against whose standard? If I was absolutely, ruthlessly honest with myself, stripped away all self-pity, examined all the evidence I could locate, then concluded something — even if it was that I couldn't conclude anything — then that conclusion would be the rock on which I would found my life from then on. The possibility for error was clear to me, but I thought, over and over again, such is the nature of being a human being. If I am wrong, and to the extent that I am, so is everybody else. One can only do what one can do, and I was giving my life, my body, my intellect over to the effort. I would accept the responsibility for more mistakes, for from now on they would be my own and nobody else's.

The more sense I made of my own truncated, incoherent and casual ideas about life, the more I put them into the context of accepted thought on the subject, of the Great Ideas, all this going on against a background of loneliness, solitude and the struggle to understand myself, ironically, the more despairing I grew.

One morning after seven years here, I awoke and remembered that I had had a strange dream. I couldn't remember what had happened before or after; all I could remember was a word which I saw clearly printed across a pale dream sky. It was "anomie."

I hadn't a clue what the word meant; I was not even sure that it was a word. But in the dream and as I awakened I was filled with such penetrating loneliness, such absolute coldness and emptiness, that my very soul was chilled.

I told myself with a grim determination rather characteristic of me, If I dreamt it, I must know what it means. At the ranch there was only an elementary school dictionary. The word was not in it. At the hay farm I had an old Funk and Wagnall's College Dictionary. It was not in there either. I pondered, a sense of the word's familiarity growing stronger. I thought I knew the word was a technical term, and from sociology in which my first husband had once been a graduate student.

Slowly over the next few weeks it came back to me: it meant, I was sure, a profound alienation from the surrounding culture. This was hardly news. But during my waking hours I tried to fight it off with all my strength, kept it well buried, so that I wouldn't consciously feel what seemed to be the hopelessness of my situation. Now I was frightened by the almost unbearable depth of the sorrow and loneliness that had been brought to the surface by the dream, so that I could no longer deny it.

I was in constant pain, tumult roared inside me. I had waited for the moment when I would awaken, and when it came, slowly, not in the flash most thinkers claimed it would, it was worse, not better. I thought only dying made sense, for without illusion it seemed to me that not only was life unbearable, it was purposeless, ugly and desolate.

Feeling myself about to implode with all that ceaseless mental activity churning around, endlessly chasing itself without an outlet, I had begun to talk to myself. If people had heard me, they'd have thought I was crazy, but it saved me from worse: screaming to the sky or banging my head against fence posts.

The house was empty and quiet. Sometimes I put on records and danced to them as I had in clubs and at parties with all my dear old friends: the Pointer Sisters, Janis Joplin, Bette Midler, "When a Man Loves a Woman," Carly Simon, James Taylor, Stevie Wonder, and going far back to the Mamas and the Papas, "Dancing in the Street." It was small comfort; it was no comfort at all.

I didn't turn to Peter. This was my own struggle, and it was too profound, too wholly and intimately mine, to turn to anyone else. Had I been in a city, I might have sought out an analyst, but I wasn't in the city, and as it was I knew this was a labor I had to complete myself, in my own way and on my own terms. It was not something Peter had ever gone through; I suspected that if I told him, he wouldn't be able to understand because his own life was so clear, so satisfying and psychically untroubled. Possibly I was a little ashamed of my own pain, which was taking place in the midst of the abundantly good life that I had been fortunate to find but with which I wasn't satisfied, because I was too inadequate a human being.

Day after day, as long as the weather allowed and I was well, I walked the roads and the fields, searching for clues in the susuration of the wind in the grass and in the boundless layers of sky. Hawks, eagles, gophers, antelope, the occasional badger, small garter snakes, coyotes running the line between earth and sky, river carp drifting with a kind of ease filled with unleashed power, the beaver and the muskrat — I waited for them to speak to me; I was looking for hints, for clues, for explanations, above all, for consolation.

During all of this I never considered leaving, or rather I considered leaving every second of every day and always found such a departure unimaginable. Returning to my old life was no longer possible, but when I looked around and told myself, This is my home; this is my home till I die, that, too, seemed equally unimaginable.

And yet, in the midst of all this turmoil and misery, I was writing novels and short stories, all of them informed by my personal struggle and conversely informing me, as I worked to give shape to my experiences so I could write them down. And if I walked every day and studied the landscape, the weather, the animals, trying to fit them into a life-scheme I could live with, I was also learning about Nature and, thus, about rural life.

THE SUBTLETY OF LAND

Some years later, when I was an established author, I said to a Toronto reporter who had asked me a question about him, "My husband is a true rural man."

"What does that mean?" the reporter asked, his voice full of skepticism.

"It means," I said, "that he understands the world in terms of wild things." I was a little surprised myself at my answer, having been called upon to explain something that until that moment had seemed self-evident, and realizing that, caught off guard, I had hit on the heart of the matter.

The reporter's pencil stopped moving, his eyes shifted away from me, he reflected, his eyes shifted back to me, and without writing anything down he changed the subject. When I told this story to a writer-naturalist friend, he said, laughing, that for the reporter my answer "does not compute."

A true rural person must be somebody born and raised on the land, outside of towns, and far from most other people. That being a given, then it follows that such life experience must result in an intrinsic understanding of the world different from that of someone raised in the cement, asphalt, glass and crowds of the city. Peter's thinking about the world was different from mine in ways that went beyond our different sexes or our different lifestyles. Where I had been trained to understand human nature from Freud and pop psychology, and the functioning of the world from classes in political economy and in history, that is, from formal education, Peter's starting point was what he had all his life lived in the midst of — it was Nature.

As years on the ranch passed, though, I began to learn from Nature too; I began to catch a glimpse of the world as he saw it through my own life in Nature. When that began to happen, a new understanding slowly, very slowly, began to dawn on me about what a life in Nature teaches one. I began to see that there might be more at the root of this difference in understanding of how the world works than I had guessed at, thinking it had to do only with simple, surface matters, like understanding cattle behavior well enough to predict their next move, or knowing the habits of antelope, or reading the sky with accuracy. I didn't yet have any idea what this deeper knowledge might be, but I watched Peter closely and tried to see what he saw.

While he was doing the spring irrigation at the hay farm, he would sometimes come across fawns only a few days old lying in the hay where they'd been left by their mothers who had gone off to forage. More than once he came to the house to get me so I could see the little spotted creature for myself.

"Watch," he would say. "When they're this young they don't even move when you come near them." Then he would bend down, pick up the trusting fawn in his arms, carry it to the closest grass-covered dike, and place it gently down where the irrigation water couldn't reach it. I worried about the mother locating her baby, but he said, with the confidence born of experience, "Don't worry. It won't take her a minute to find him." When we went back hours later the fawn would always be gone. These and other incidents reminded me over and over again that Peter, and other rural people who knew no other landscape, had formed his attitude to the prairie and his understanding of its weather, its growth patterns and its animals by a lifetime of immersion in it.

In my reading and occasionally in conversation with urban visitors, I read or hear people either saying directly or implying indirectly that *true rural* people don't notice or appreciate the beauty in which they live. Although I don't say so, the arrogance and ignorance of such remarks always makes me angry, implying as it does that rural people lack humanity, are somehow an inferior branch of the human species, that beauty is beyond their ken. It is one thing to come from the city and be overwhelmed by the beauty of Nature and to speak of it, and another thing entirely to have lived in it so long that it has seeped into your bones and your blood and is inseparable from your own being, so that it is part of you and requires no mention or hymns of praise.

Peter preferred to do our annual spring and fall cattle drives on horseback, a trek which took three days. Bringing the cattle down to the valley around Christmastime could be very unpleasant and then it was often hard to get help, so that we sometimes made that move with only Peter, me and one other person. But three days out on the prairie during a warm spring were paradise; we never had any trouble rounding up enough riders then. If the spring move was usually a joy, the best part of it was the eight to ten miles of unbroken prairie without even any true roads through it that we used to cross each time.

I knew the first time Peter took me across those miles of prairie that I loved to be there far from towns or even houses, on native shortgrass that had never been broken, where the grass hadn't been overgrazed and was full of birds' nests in the spring, and long-eared jackrabbits as big as small dogs, antelope in the distance, and coyotes that often followed us singing all the way.

Of course, unless she's a dyed-in-the-wool, bona fide horse-and-cattlewoman herself, when it's time to move cattle, and especially if there are adolescent sons on the place, the rancher's wife usually gets stuck driving the truck. The rancher is the one with the understanding of the cattle, knowledge of the route, and the cattle-management skills. As boss and owner, he has to ride. If there are adolescents along, it's taken for granted that they'll ride because they have to learn, which has a high priority on Saskatchewan ranches, and because it's so much fun and nobody wants to deprive kids of a little harmless fun.

The rancher's wife packs the meals, stows them in the truck, serves them when the time comes and packs up after. She carries drinking water and coffee and the extra jackets or the ones taken off when the day gets too warm. She carries tack, fencing pliers and other tools, and sometimes, if the move is just before calving begins, she'll have a newborn in the back of the truck and often several of them, each one marked in some way — maybe a colored string around its neck — so it can be returned to the right mother every few hours. As the drive wears on, she's likely to have exhausted adolescents in the cab with her, while their horses are either driven ahead or led by one of the men from his own horse. Usually, at some point, somebody will take pity on her and spell her off for an hour or so, so that she can get out into the fresh air and ride a little herself.

When you move cattle you move, depending on the weather, at the leisurely pace of about two miles an hour. For long stretches you don't need to speak at all, and you can ride a mile or more away from any other rider if you want to. As you ride, the prairie slowly seeps into you. I have never felt such pure, unadulterated joy in simple existence as I have felt at moments out on the prairie during the spring move.

Ordinarily I wouldn't get to ride until we were close to the ranch and our helpers went home. Then Peter and I changed our headquarters from the hay farm to the ranch house and we'd ride horses out to the cattle to bring them the rest of the way home. Occasionally, he'd have someone along who didn't ride and who would drive the truck so that I could ride. Most of the time, though, I reluctantly drove the truck and kept my fingers crossed for a chance either to ride or, as I sometimes did, to walk leading Peter's horse — for me to ride him was unthinkable, the very thought making my stomach turn over and my knees quake — while Peter spelled me off in the driver's seat.

Nowadays we calve at the hay farm instead of at the ranch, mostly because it's easier to keep an eye on the cows, but also because there's shelter for them here during the inevitable calf-killing spring storms. Often, too, in spring there is no water in the ditches or fields along the way and, of course, the cattle must have water each day, moving or not. If we calve at the hay farm — Peter not being a believer in early calving — by the time we're ready to move in late April most of the farmers along the route have seeded their crops. The traditional mistrust between farmers and ranchers being what it is, it would be dangerous if one cow strayed one foot from the road allowances, those which, usually without bothering to get permission from the municipality, farmers haven't plowed up and seeded to wheat. And cows being what they are, you never know when one might take it into her head to head out, calf at her side, racing for Alaska or Mexico across a newly seeded field with a couple of cowboys in hot pursuit. Guns have been pointed on such occasions. Nowadays, it hardly seems worth the risk.

During one of the last spring moves we made, Peter had had more people along than he'd expected and before we'd gone very far he'd given one of the kids my horse, which he'd been leading, to ride. Not long after that, he'd given my saddle — the only one with stirrups that could be shortened enough for small people — to another teenager to use. I had reconciled myself to not being able to ride on this move. I could still look at the landscape, I could roll down the window and smell the sweet air and feel the breeze and the sun on my face, and occasionally I could stop, get out, and stroll around a bit in the grass.

We always made it a practice to stop for a meal when we reached that stretch of pure unbroken prairie. The riders would dismount and hobble their horses or tie them to the fence, I'd park the truck, Peter would throw down a couple of hay bales for a table or for people to sit on, and I'd put out the lunch. We'd sit in the sun and eat sandwiches, and his mother's baked beans, the pot wrapped in layers of newspapers to keep it warm, and drink coffee from thermoses. Long before we reached there I'd have begun to look forward to that moment.

I discovered what the annual day spent crossing these acres of prairie meant to me when, as we were about to begin that part of the trip, a circumstance arose — I don't even remember what it was — that meant somebody had to drive one of the men the twenty or so miles around the fields, down the roads and wait with him there at the corrals for the riders and cattle to arrive. Since Peter could hardly order anybody else to do it, and nobody volunteered, it was taken for granted that as his wife I would leave the drive and take this man where he needed to go.

I wanted to protest, but I couldn't bring myself to do it in front of so many people, especially since arguing or complaining are just not done on a trip like that. It would be a little like a sailor telling the captain of a ship that he didn't feel like taking the watch that night. My true feelings were too private to speak out loud, and I couldn't come up with any practical reason why I shouldn't have to that didn't hint of adolescent pique or, not knowing how the others felt about the prairie — but the fact that nobody volunteered to go should have given me a hint — that I could be sure anybody but Peter would understand. And everyone else was a volunteer; I was official staff. I knew I wouldn't be able to go back and catch up with the drive, either. For me, for that year, the drive was over.

I got back in the truck and started driving, trying to smile, trying to make conversation, while all the time I was fighting back tears. I wanted so badly to spend that last few hours on the prairie, the only time we ever went through those fields, that I had an actual pain in my chest as I drove away and that stayed with me till I went to bed that night.

I said about that incident much later to a friend, "If everything happens to teach you something, why was that taken away from me? What was I supposed to learn from that?" and answered myself, "To teach me how much the wild prairie means to me." Years later, I was able to go further: to understand how precious it is, how unique, how deeply it might affect one, changing even one's understanding of life.

Sometimes I think I'm still not over that loss. Especially since, during the good times, farmers bought all that land the rest of the gang traveled over on horseback that day, and plowed it up to turn it into a farm. Now, ten years later, the farming operation is failing, but you can't turn plowed-up short-grass prairie back into the original terrain. It's gone forever, or given a human life span, as good as forever, along with the wildlife that lived on it.

It occurs to me now to wonder if perhaps the very real — and surprising even to me — sorrow I felt that day as I drove away, and all the rest of the day and for days afterward, wasn't perhaps intuitive, if perhaps a part of me knew that I would never again experience the sweetness of that air, the sun warm on my face and hands, the view so vast the soul felt free, because by the next spring or the spring after that it would be gone forever.

As the years passed, I felt more and more that the best comfort I had was in being in the landscape. I was only mildly curious about how the prairie was formed, and when and how it was evolving, and I certainly had none of the interests of ecologists or environmentalists. I was merely looking at the prairie as a human being, savoring it for its beauty which engaged all the senses and brought with it a feeling of well-being, contentment and often even joy.

My approach was to simply wander in it with no particular destination, to lie in the sun and bury my nose in the sweet-smelling grasses and forbs such as sage, to admire the colors and textures of the sedges, shrubs and succulents which make up the mixed grass prairie, or to sit on a slope looking out across miles of prairie to the horizon, watching the shifting of shadows and light across it, thinking no thoughts that, a moment later, I would remember. I was there only to enjoy the prairie. I asked for nothing more, not thinking there was anything more.

I had only the most cursory interest in the names of the plants, although Peter's mother taught me a few of those which flowered: scarlet mallow, three-flowered avens, gumbo primrose, golden bean, which she called "buffalo bean," and which someone else told me she knew as the wild sweet pea. I could hardly miss the wild rose or the prairie sunflower, and I knew a few others such as the wild licorice and the wild morning glory and anemones which grow along the riverbank, from my childhood in the north. Peter showed me the greasewood, badger bush and club moss and pointed out the two species of cactus — the prickly pear and the pincushion — and much later I learned from a rancher's wife (herself a rancher and also a poet) that if you had the patience to gather the berries, you could make cactus-berry jelly. I taught myself a few: the many types of cinquefoil and sage, and milkweed, and the Canada thistle with its purple flower that a saddle horse — "Watch this," Peter said — would clip tidily off with its bared teeth, never touching a barb. I longed to see a field of wild prairie lilies as I had in my childhood in the north, but I never have, not even a single flower growing wild in the grass.

Because we had a hay farm, I learned to identify a number of grasses — timothy, bromegrass, foxtail — and legumes — clover, alfalfa — which I saw every day, some of which were imported species, crested wheat grass, Russian wild rye, and many of which, like reed canary grass, were very beautiful. I attended three day-long range schools with Peter, one in the Bears Paw Mountains of Montana, but I did so chiefly for the adventure and to spend an entire day on the prairie instead of only a few hours. At these schools I learned to identify death camas when I saw it, and a few of the many native species of grass — needle-and-thread grass, June grass, blue grama or buffalo grass — and a forb or two.

Other seasons brought different pleasures. All one snowy winter I walked a mile down the riverbed every morning with the dog trotting ahead, flushing out cattle from the banks or far back around the last curve where the fenceline crossed and stopped them, then chasing them up to the feed-grounds where Peter and his hired man were throwing out hay, grain bales and grain itself. For two winters the snow was so deep that it muffled sound so that the cattle which had sought shelter in these snug places couldn't hear the tractor and didn't come out for feed. Or sometimes, looking back, I think Peter came and got me each morning to make that walk out of understanding that I needed to feel useful, a part of the operation, and that if I spent all of each day inside that tiny log house I would soon be "bushed," develop cabin fever, be impossible to live with — that I might leave.

I remember those walks each morning as among the best of my life. I would head down the riverbed, following in the tracks of the cattle where the snow was too deep to walk comfortably in. The banks of the river are high and steep, and the winds had pushed the snow into deep banks that overhung the edges of the cliffsides in fat lips of snow that looked like waves on the ocean and from which long icicles sometimes hung. Looking up from the snowy riverbed, I saw white walls of snow and then the snowy billows and beyond them the brilliant sky. I saw the places where partridges snuggled up for the night to keep warm and followed the tracks of coyotes and foxes and animals whose tracks I didn't recognize. I was picking up knowledge, hardly even noticing that was what I was doing. Running to cut off a cow, I fell headlong in the snow and, with no one watching me, lay there laughing, blinking up at the sky, losing myself in its blue depths.

For most people the worse the weather is, the more likely they are to stay indoors; not so for old-fashioned ranchers — for them the worse the weather, the more likely the rancher is to be out in it, in the midst of blizzards searching for cattle out on the prairie and chasing them down into the shelter of deep coulees, or home to the windbreaks and corrals. On such days I went along with Peter and learned again that the human limits of endurance are much greater than day-to-day life has us believe; that is, I became less afraid of the weather at the same time as I became a good deal more respectful of it.

One of the first Christmas gifts Peter gave me was a pair of cross-country skis, and as long as there was enough snow, which there usually isn't in this desert country, I'd be out on the prairie in the winter, too, skiing. I began to take my skis and go out into the hills during storms, having discovered that I liked storms for the way they changed the appearance of familiar places and for the sense of mystery they brought to them.

Memories of my childhood came back to me: playing in the bush with my friends, with my sisters and cousins in our grandmother's garden, skating on frozen sloughs in winter till the pain from the cold became so bad even we kids couldn't stand it anymore and went home, the winter we had built a snow fort that lasted for months as we added on and made it more and more substantial so that it stood well into spring. I felt like a child again, had fleeting moments when I remembered how wonderful the world itself had once seemed, and how it was to be cared for, worry-free, and living in the body again and not just the mind.

And I was recreating myself as a writer. I not only was meditative by nature, this having been developed in me as the result of being an extremely shy and retiring child in a big family, I had also developed in me the seeds of the observer. It was a lucky thing, although I'd never have admitted it then, to have arrived a stranger in a strange land, when I was no longer young, with a touch of the observer's cold eye already in my makeup.

I found myself observing the very people with whom I seemed to have so little in common. I saw the people of my new community as different from those of the rest of the province, and I was surprised to discover that they themselves seemed to define themselves as different, although nobody ever explicitly said so, in that they often had closer links both in terms of lifestyle and in family ties to Alberta and to Montana than they did to Saskatchewan. Many of the families had begun as Americans and had close relatives on the farms and ranches over the border and in Alberta, and when young people went off to higher education or trades schools or to jobs, when I first came here, they were much more likely to go to Alberta than to Saskatoon or even Regina. As a group they seemed to me often to think more like western Americans or like Albertans, with that essentially conservative, independent cast of mind, than they did like the good-old-Tommy-Douglas-prairie-socialist school of thought to which I belonged and which had always seemed to me to define Saskatchewan.

I soon discovered, in my attempt to tell the story of these people and this place, that my fund of facts, of precise knowledge, was inadequate to the task I'd set myself. Each story, each book, each play would become an exercise in information gathering. When Peter couldn't answer my questions I turned to books. Peter took me to meet old people, old men who'd pioneered in the area, and I listened to their stories and made notes, and where it was possible, which was practically never, I tried to match their memories to the scant written history I could find.

I carried a notebook everywhere. Chasing cows home on bitter winter days, I'd stop the truck, get out, draw a little diagram of the way an animal had pushed away the snow from a sage bush, write a description of the bush and the snow and the droppings the animal had left, the colors, the place where the sun was in the sky on that day at that time and how the cattle looked. I wrote the last few pages of *The Gates of the Sun* sitting on a straw bale in the back of the pickup in a neighbor's field while I waited for Peter to finish baling the straw, pausing in my scribbling only to ask questions of Peter and the neighbor, when they stopped for coffee, about what was a native species, whether bird, animal or plant, and what wasn't. It constantly amazed me how much the men knew.

With every story and every book I was forced to search out new information. My fund of information, of facts, obtained in all these ways — my own observations, Peter's answers to my incessant questions, the stories of old people, books — was growing. Without intending to or even really wanting to, I was becoming knowledgeable about the history of the area and its plant and animal life. Although I will never know all there is to know — Peter still knows a thousand times more than I do — having begun by being transported by its beauty, and then being overwhelmed by my sense of loneliness and purposelessness, I was at last starting to feel at home in the terrain, at home in the landscape. Of course, I didn't see this as it was happening, but by learning to name things in my new environment, by discovering the scheme of the place and the way the parts fit together, I was making them my own, and by this I was slowly healing myself.

Years later when I was the expert instead of the neophyte, a friend and I were out walking in the rain. In this semiarid country where rain is rare and precious, walking in it is exhilarating, imbued even with a touch of magic. We came to a place where a pair of great horned owls sat watching us, and as my friend went closer to see them better, I sat in the grass in my leaky boots and a borrowed yellow rain jacket which came to my knees, not minding the wet, looking out over the misty fields, noticing how everything smelled different because of the moisture, how colors had changed and intensified.

I thought of how my friend and I had moved over the wet ground, where we had gone and not gone, what we had found ourselves doing, and suddenly I realized that it was the land — Nature — that had guided our steps, made our choices for us, and not the other way around. That is, because we were friends and rambling in the countryside for the pleasure of each other's company and for the pleasure of being out-of-doors, having no set plan or goal, we had gone where the shape of the land had suggested itself to us; we had done what the land had made available to us. If it was too muddy or wet in one place, we went somewhere else; if a hill was too steep, we went around; there was no way to cross the river without swimming and it was too cold to swim, so we followed its course instead and sat on its bank.

I thought, then said, "This land makes Crees of us all." By this, I meant that it appeared to me that the Crees, for example, developed the culture they developed because it was the best fit between themselves and the land. And it was the *land* that taught them that. They adapted to the land, and not the other way around as we Europeans so stupidly did, trying to force this arid western land to be, as government propaganda had for seventy-five years and more put it, "the breadbasket of the world."

I began to think about the ways in which land affects the individual, or at least this particular landscape, the Great Plains of North America. I began to see that in our human arrogance we assume we can affect the land but it can't affect us — except in practical ways: hurricanes, floods, drought — when there are plenty of ways we might find that the land — Nature — is affecting us without our being aware of it. In considering the differences between Peter and myself, I had not imagined or considered the possibility that he had been shaped by the land, by Nature, that in subtle ways we've never identified nor even really talked about, his psyche itself had been shaped by Nature not merely by *his* observations of *it* but by its subtle, never described or even consciously realized, influence on *him*.

The Great Plains landscape is an elemental one. There is little natural water in the form of lakes or rivers or even ponds, no forests, no mountains — just miles and miles of land and a sky across which weather visibly, majestically passes. One winter visitor to this place said it reminded him of the high Arctic where he had once lived, and several others, Wallace Stegner included, spoke of the plains of Africa. The landscape is so huge that our imaginations can't contain it or outstrip it, and the climate is concomitantly arbitrary and severe.

It is geology stripped bare, leaving behind only a vast sky and land stretched out in long, sweeping lines that blend into the distant horizon with a line that is sometimes so clear and sharp it is surreal, and sometimes exists at the edge of metaphysics, oscillating in heat waves or, summer or winter, blending into mirages and the realm of dreams and visions which wavers just the other side of the horizon. The Great Plains are a land for visionaries, they induce visions, they are themselves visions, the line between fact and dream is so blurred. What other landscape around the world produces the mystic psyche so powerfully? Sky and land, that is all, and grass, and what Nature leaves bare the human psyche fills.

It was not until I moved into the country to live that my significant dreaming really began. I did not think about this fact, but if I had, I am sure I would have explained it as a by-product of the radical change in my way of life. Eventually it was suggested to me by an eminent western Canadian writer in whom I had confided that perhaps living in this ancient, skeletal landscape had brought on these dreams. At the time I reserved judgment, but a few years later, in another context, another western Canadian writer told me how she had, after years of living in the city where she didn't believe she had dreamt at all, moved out into the country and suddenly began having vivid, meaningful dreams. She attributed these to the influence of the landscape in which she now made her home.

In the context of these remarks it seems to me very significant that dreams have always held an important place in Aboriginal cultures of the Great Plains of North America, as they have in many other such cultures around the world. Aboriginal people take the content of their dreams as simply another source of information about the world, a guide for action, and as prophecy, either in their individual lives or as directives to their communities. In these cultures it is considered extemely foolish, a great insult, even a sin, to ignore an important dream.

Prophetic dreams are accepted at face value and are used as a basis for action. A South Dakota writer living near Rapid City told me that a few years ago Chief Crazy Horse — whose name I'm told should more accurately be translated as "Enchanted Horse," or "Vision Horse" — appeared in dreams to the elders of his nation to warn them about an imminent flood on a branch of the Cheyenne River. The flood did occur and it killed more than a hundred of his people who lived along its banks. Hugh Brody, in *Maps and Dreams*, describes a hunting culture, the Beaver Indians of northeastern British Columbia, where the best hunters are guided by dreams to their kill; the very best hunter-dreamers have even dreamt the way to heaven and then, awaking, have drawn the map.

Although I sometimes go for long stretches without any dreams that seem important to me, a few years ago I began to have the occasional prophetic dream myself. I dreamt the San Francisco earthquake a couple of weeks before it happened. Since I'd never been to San Francisco, I thought the city in the dream was Vancouver and the broken bridge, the Lions' Gate. Although it was a powerful enough dream to tell people about it, I certainly never took it as prophecy until I saw the broken span of the bridge on television. It was identical to the one in my dream where it had been the main icon. I dreamt of the Japanese airplane that lost its rudder and, after weaving drunkenly through the air for half an hour, crashed into a mountain. I was in bed dreaming it as it was happening.

When I got up the first thing Peter did was to tell me about this terrible event that had just happened in Japan. I even dreamt of the death of one of the Russian Communist leaders a few days before he died. It may be that I've had more prophetic dreams than I know but simply haven't remembered. Actually I think this may be true of everyone, but most people don't record their dreams as I usually do, and so forget them.

I have described the dream I had in which a giant eagle and a giant owl appeared to me. It became for me a life-dream, a significant dream that launched me on a journey through comparative religion, mythology, the study of dreams, psychoanalysis, and finally into the study of the nature of the female. At an archetypal level, it is a dream about masculine power, symbolized by the soaring eagle, and feminine power, symbolized by the owl standing near me on the ground. In beauty and power they are exactly equal, but I, a woman, had spent my life to this point following the eagle — that is, accepting masculine interpretations of life in general and, of my own life, accepting masculine goals and taking masculine desires for my own — instead of cleaving to the owl, searching out and coming to terms with my own feminine soul.

My search for understanding of the dream led me into and through my novel *Luna* — the story of the lives of contemporary ranch and farm women and how they live, feel about, and understand their rural, agricultural, traditional lives — and from there into my short story collection *Fever*, a much more personal and urbanized study of the same issues. It's been a good dozen years since I had that dream and I still run across further ways to interpret it. Not only have I accepted it as guidance in the direction my life has taken, it is, to a degree, the foundation on which I have built the rest of my life.

I think that significant dreaming is one way in which Nature influences and changes the individual, developing in her/him an awareness of Nature as more than mere locale, or a setting, a context, as more than beauty, as more than something that is merely Other.

It was in Joseph Campbell's *Primitive Mythology* that I first heard of Aboriginal dreamtime, and, not long after, in a much more firsthand and compelling way in *The Lost World of the Kalahari* by Laurens van der Post. All peoples of the earth have creation stories of one kind or another. The stories of prescientific peoples tell variously of a time when the world was in the process of being created along with the creatures on it. This was a timeless time, a time before time, when animals, plants and people could become one another and the formations of the earth were taking shape. It is called, in mythologies around the world, dreamtime, and out of it springs stories and legends about archetypal creatures, sometimes gods, whose manifestations remain now in the fallen time.

It seems, too, that on some level this timeless time still exists in another realm, and those people peculiarly blessed — including, but never exclusively, shamans — may still go there. In this realm many strange things can happen: animals can converse with humans and vice versa; the dead may appear and speak, or creatures from the dreamtime thought by some of us to be merely metaphoric. The earth becomes more beautiful, approaches, even achieves, perfection, and everything in it and on it is imbued with meaning. And especially the sense of the ticking of time vanishes.

I believe that since Aboriginal people around the world have non-technological cultures and live in and by Nature — or at least, once did when their cultures were developing — and these cultures had developed the concept of dreamtime and took dreaming very seriously whether in New Zealand, Australia, the Kalahari Desert of Africa, or the Great Plains of North America, that surely it was Nature which, whether with will and intention or not, taught, allowed, gave them dreams as an instrument of knowledge.

I began to see from my own experience living in it that the land and the wild creatures who live in it and on it, and the turning of the earth, the rising and setting of the sun and the moon, and the constant passing of weather across its surface — that is, Nature — influenced rural people to make them what they are, more than even they knew.

Close proximity to a natural environment — being in Nature — alters all of us in ways which remain pretty much unexplored, even undescribed in our culture. I am suggesting that these ways in which such a closeness affects us, from dreams to more subtle and less describable phenomena, are real, and that we should stop thinking, with our inflated human egos, that all the influence is the other way around. We might try to shift our thinking in this direction so that we stop blithely improving the natural world around us, and begin to learn, as Aboriginal people have, what Nature in her subtle but powerful manner has to teach us about how to live.

More and more I am coming to believe that our alienation from the natural world is at root of much that has gone so wrong in the modern world, and that if Nature has anything to teach us at all, her first lesson is in humility.

STONES IN THE GRASS

As I write this, on the shelf in front of me sits a chunk of wine-colored rock. It is probably sandstone, although rock identification is not something I've expended much energy on since it is not in my nature to be obsessed with what natural objects themselves are made of, or how or when, or what their proper names might be. Although I had wanted to learn the names of plants and animals I saw every day, a more scientific approach otherwise is not only irrelevant to my reasons for going out into Nature but I think too often the effort to find the answers only distracts from what is really to be found there.

This little rock is an oblong about four and a half inches by two and a half. The smooth, curved surface of its underside, still in its natural state, makes a satisfying fit to the curve of my palm. Its upper surface is rough and one rim has been carefully chipped to make a curved, sharp scraping edge. I can still see clearly the little indentations in the stone, probably made by another stone. Because of its warm wine color — most of these I find on the hills around here are chipped out of murky tan-colored chert — and because it is so clearly what it is, it is especially beautiful. But beyond that, I cherish it because it holds personal meaning for me.

A writer friend had come for a visit, and knowing from his writings and his conversation that he and I shared a similar point of view about Nature, I took him for a walk to the particular field, my favorite, I've mentioned. We hadn't been there, strolling, talking, five minutes, when suddenly he bent. At the same time as he bent I felt something strong in my chest and I said, as he lifted that small wine-colored piece of rock, "That looks like a scraper," at the same moment as he said, holding it up, "It's a scraper."

It was as though we had found it together, although he was the one who first saw it and bent and picked it up. Yet that something in my chest told me what he had found before I saw it, at the moment he was bending and lifting it. His find astonished me. "That's the first artifact anyone has found here," I said. "I've never found anything," although I hadn't been looking, since searching for spear or arrow points, stone hammers or pounders or scrapers, weapons and tools left behind by Aboriginal people is also irrelevant to my reasons for going there.

We examined it, touched it, exclaimed over its beauty and the fact that we had entered the land and found it, virtually together, as if the land had meant us to find it, as some sort of affirmation of . . . what? Us? Him? Some venture we might expect to engage in together? We didn't know and we didn't speculate. The event, although it raised questions, seemed significant enough in itself for us to regard it as a blessing and to let it go at that. "It feels like it wants to stay here," the writer said, and dropped it back into the place where we'd found it. He didn't ask me if I thought it should stay there, but I accepted what he had said and was silent as he replaced it. But I didn't forget it, and now, because the scraper has taken on new meaning, I suspect he was wrong.

When it first occurred to me that I might write this book, I thought the idea as impossible as I had the day more than fifteen years before when I first thought I might write a novel. I spent a year vacillating, trying to talk myself out of doing what I couldn't stop thinking about until it had entered the realm of obsession. At last I succumbed.

When I was ready, I sat down at my desk and typed *The Perfection of the Morning*, then waited in that state of suspension of writers like me, of held breath, obliviousness to one's surroundings, the moment fraught with tension and with prayer, a kind of intense concentration not on some particular but on emptying oneself so that the right words might have room to form. And then, as so far has always happened, ideas began to flow, to shape themselves into words, sentences, paragraphs, as I typed.

A strange thing began to happen. I began to have a powerful sense of that same field where we had found the scraper, hovering all around me at the far range of my vision. I could see without looking its green-tinted grassy hills and plains, the multihued rocks, the greasewood, sage, badger and wild rose bushes growing in the clefts of its hills. But it was more than that: it felt as it feels when I am there — I felt enveloped in that aura or presence, which on good days is as if I have entered the sway of another consciousness, as if I am not alone but watched over by a presence much bigger than I am. It was as though that presence or landscape had incarnated and come to me as I sat in my office far from it.

I tried to shake it, to blink it away, to relegate it to the realm of imagination. It refused to go, and I saw I hadn't induced it. Awe rose in my chest, heat flushed my face. I thought, this — the writing down of it after all that grappling with whether I should or could — must be the right thing to do. I sat and felt what I knew to be a vision blossom into its full shape around me. I waited for what I wasn't sure: for the breath of cool wind on my cheek carrying with it the sweet, peppery scent of sage, for a voice to speak.

One always asks too much of these small mysteries. In a moment the vision I was seeing faded and I was left with the work in the typewriter before me. But something had happened, something rare and beautiful. My task now seemed laden with purpose, indeed, a trust of some sort. I thought of my wounded spirit coyote; I thought of my soaring eagle spirit and of the solidity and beauty of my earthbound owl. Surely, I felt, there had to be a connection, and as I pondered them I realized the three visions had all to do with Nature — were visions of Nature. I felt blessed by these visions, and that I had to act on them, if I could see how I should act. I had no doubt I must write my book — the spirit coyote had looked meaningfully directly at me; the hills had hovered around me, as if to encourage me. If I could make no direct connection with the owl and the eagle, I didn't worry about it.

But, having finally gotten up the courage to start writing this book, a leap of faith if ever there was one, I found, after a week's work, that I wasn't sure where to go next, or that I had said all that needed to be said up to that point. I was in need of sustenance and inspiration, and so I left my desk to go walking in the field where we'd found the scraper.

I walked and climbed, and sat and thought, and tried to clear my mind to make room for whatever it was I needed that no matter how hard I struggled my conscious mind hadn't been able to produce. Finally, I came to the place which I think of as the focal point of the field. There I sat down with a panorama of fields and hills spread out below me, and concentrated, going over my reasons for trying to write this book, reminding myself of them, and reassessing them to see if they still made sense to me.

My reasons still held; I had no sense that I should give the book up, although the problem of where to go next in it was still unsolved. But I knew, as I've always known with each book, that the best parts aren't pieces that I imagine myself, at least that's not how I conceive of them. They seem instead to come in a split second of insight, as if the inside of my body were, at such times, a darkened theater into which a shaft of wisdom, some visionary light, suddenly is thrust before the light goes quickly out again. Those blessed moments come best to me when, after a night of vivid dreaming, I get up and go straight to my work, or the state of mind which produces them can come from reading the work of a great writer, or — and this was why I was out in the field — they can be induced by solitary wandering, day after day, across the land in her natural state.

On this day, frustrated in my writing and going back to the book's beginnings in silence and alone, sitting in the grass overlooking a vast landscape barely peopled, but marked everywhere it hadn't been plowed with the signs of centuries of crossings of unknown humans, feeling some pure connection to the universe, I hoped for a sign that would act as a stamp of approval, as had the small vision that came to me the morning I'd begun to write.

Never ask for a sign, I muttered to myself; how heartless, fickle and inscrutable are the gods; you never get signs when you need them, and when you do, you can't understand them; besides, you're probably crazy.

I thought, although I doubted anything at all would happen, that a sign *could* consist of my finding on my return journey through the land something to take away with me, which I normally never do. By "something" I meant an especially beautiful or unusual rock that I hadn't seen before, or maybe even an arrow or spear point. I set out in a direction that would take me back roughly in a straight line to what I think of as the exit, my head down, watching the ground, occasionally looking up to check my bearings. It wasn't the easiest route by any means, since I had chosen to climb hills and descend them when it would have been easier to go around them.

Despite my efforts to take the direct route, I somehow managed to stray a little from it, because suddenly there in front of my shoes was that little wine-colored scraper the writer and I had deliberately left behind and which I had seen on every subsequent trip onto the land, but always left exactly where we'd found it.

I thought, Now there's a sign if ever I saw one. There are, after all, more than a hundred and fifty acres in that field and I am one very small person and I wasn't even thinking about that scraper or its location, in fact, was trying to go somewhere else. So I picked it up and brought it home with me, after telling it and myself that I would put it back when my book was finished. It would be my talisman.

Although occasionally I have found fossils and concretions in other places, this was the first scraper I had ever found — the first removable piece of evidence of human occupation prior to that of the ranchers and then the farmers. Now, as I grow to know the land better, I become more and more aware that wherever nobody picked the rocks and plowed the land, it is still strewn with signs of the nomadic camps of Aboriginal people, indicated by lost or abandoned stone artifacts of one kind or another.

In the West in general and Saskatchewan in particular, where, according to the 1986 census, eight percent of the population claims part or all ancestry as Aboriginal — and it is thought that there is a significant number more who don't know or else choose not to report this ancestry — Native people are very much a presence in most of the villages, towns and cities. My earliest memories, going back fifty years to the days of our life in the bush when my father ran a small sawmill, included the presence of Native people who had sometimes camped in their tepees in a small meadow nearby while the men worked at the mill. I remember their tepees and I remember the glimpses I caught of the faces of the men eating in the cookshack, where we "little girls," as we were referred to, weren't allowed to go, but I remember no children at all, and only the women who occasionally came to the kitchen door and talked to our mother. In their long dresses and with their strange silence, they frightened me and, much to her annoyance, when they came, I would hide behind my mother's skirt.

Native children were very much present at the convent near Prince Albert where I began school a few years later, since an orphanage for Native children in the city had burned down and many of the residents had been sent to live at our school where, according to my memories, they were shamefully treated. (Actually, the nuns showed nobody much mercy.) Later, in Melfort, although there were no Native children in our school at all that I can recall, every summer they camped in the woods on the edge of town and became a part of the tableau of town life, families rolling by in horse-drawn wagons, the women coming to the door selling berries and handmade rag rugs. Our mother and the other neighbor women reserved their strong sympathies for the women, whether rightly or wrongly, having no great regard for the men. On this subject, our father, who knew Native people firsthand as we did not, was silent.

My sisters and I were raised in the attitude that Native people had been very badly treated by our government — "men," our mother would have said — and that the conditions under which they lived were a crime. But we were poor people too — the working poor — and there wasn't anything we could do about it. This was the attitude of most European people at the time in our position, and included in it, I believe, was an unwitting and unexamined racism, a dismissal of a people. If they had had a glorious past, our families knew little of it and would not have considered it pertinent. Nor did we know anything of the Native peoples' myths, their beliefs or their attitude to the natural world. It would never have occurred to us to think they might have something to teach us about living on the prairie. In this blindness we were taught and encouraged by our schools, our churches, and our political leaders.

And the truth was, because no Native people were ever a real part of our lives as children, I at least was afraid of them. Often a gang of us would pack lunches and go off to spend the day exploring and playing in the aspen bush around the town. If the Indians were camping nearby, we would be sure to stay well away from that part of the woods, or we would not go at all. I remember one day when we misjudged where their camp was or, absorbed in our play, forgot completely that they were there, or perhaps a gang of Native boys were out exploring as we were, and stumbled across us.

We heard them coming and, before they broke through the bush, turned tail and ran for home faster, at least in my case, than I had ever run before. They chased us, although who knows what they would have done if we hadn't run (might we have gotten to know each other?) out past the edge of the bush where, looking back over our shoulders as we ran, we saw them standing — I remember that some of them were waving sticks — shouting at us.

Yet I remember a very different encounter as well: one of my sisters had been crippled very badly by polio in the epidemic of 1947, and one day a

Native woman passing by on the sidewalk and seeing her condition as we played together handed her a five-dollar bill. Having been reduced by white society to selling berries — saskatoons, blueberries, chokecherries — for a pittance, she could still find it in her heart to pity a child of her oppressors in such grievous condition, and to show her compassion with a gesture of such magnitude.

My fear — earlier of the women, and then of the boys — was grounded in nothing rational; nothing had ever happened to me to justify it. There was no place where we met Native people as equals in those days, not at school, not at play, or on the streets of the town, yet they were always there, like the forests, like the lakes and the prairie, always a part of what it was to live in Saskatchewan. Their constant presence on the fringes of our society was a dark shadow made up of equal parts guilt, which too often transmuted itself into scorn and even hatred, fear, curiosity, sympathy and shame. All of us walked in the gloom of that shadow believing, I suppose, if we thought about it at all, that one day we would be free of our guilt for what we did to them, not realizing, as I do now, that no matter how good our intentions or, indeed, our actions, many centuries and generations will have to pass before that sad history becomes no longer relevant.

In my new home, looking at the faces of the people passing by on the streets of the few towns, I was aware of a puzzling gap. One day it dawned on me what it was I was missing. When I asked why there were no Native people around, nobody had an answer beyond an uncertain shrug of the shoulders. Some I asked pointed out that there is a reserve near Maple Creek and that one might see Native people on the streets of that town, which wasn't an answer and in fact only increased the mystery.

Peter and his father had occasionally bought fence posts from the men of the reserve and had a passing acquaintance with a few of them. Since my marriage I had seen some of the young men competing in the rodeo held every July in the Cypress Hills adjacent to their land, but I knew about the reserve to the north only that it was Cree, or so I thought, and that it was very small. Because I believed the reserve to be Cree, my initial impression was that our corner of southwest Saskatchewan must once have been Cree territory.

It is plain to any inhabitant that nobody could live on land away from coulees for any length of time during much of the year, as out of them there is no shelter from wind, blizzards, thunderstorms or from the relentless summer sun, no wood for fires, and almost every summer by July nearly all the naturally collected surface water has evaporated in the intense heat. And, as has been amply documented, winters out on the open plains can be so appalling as to frighten the most intrepid westerner.

Bitter experience says it is most likely that centuries had passed without these endless miles of grass having seen any humans at all during winter. It was the mid-eighteenth century before Plains tribes, many of whom had had guns for a hundred years, acquired horses, which made it possible to go some distance from camp to obtain water or firewood. Yet I have found, as have other residents of the drier areas, stone circles and cairns, tools and points far from creeks or reliable water sources such as natural springs, which surely indicate that despite the drawbacks, people came and stayed long enough to leave behind traces, some not merely utilitarian, but whose true purpose is unknown, at least to non-Natives.

We do know that Plains people hunted buffalo, great herds of which grazed on the open plains most of the year, probably trekking south and into wooded territory for the winter months. With their guns and horses, buffalo jumps and occasional buffalo pounds, Plains people mastered the art of hunting and buffalo became not only their primary food source but were sought for their hides and put to numerous other uses. Every inch of this area must have been ridden over by buffalo-hunting Plains people, and it must have been very familiar to any number of Native hunting bands who camped here.

Although in the years since I was a student more and more scholars have begun the difficult study of the movements, alliances, life — the history — of pre-treaty Amerindian Nations, I found that the information being published is still in a form that is more than a little confusing to any but the most determined scholar. Never one to do more research than I could avoid, and four hundred kilometers from the nearest university library, I wanted nonetheless to know badly enough why there were no Native people here beyond that one small reserve in the Hills to pursue the answer. Somewhere I had heard this was Blackfoot land which, given the evidence of the reserve, puzzled me. I wanted to know what was correct, thinking that there would be one simple answer.

The first place I looked was to the great period of exploration of what is today the Prairie provinces. I found that no Europeans — at least none who left a record — traveled through the true southwest corner of this province before the mid-nineteenth century. For the most part, the early explorers followed the river systems and there was no major river south of the Saskatchewan, or the Bad River, as Peter Fidler, the first European trader-explorer to follow the South Saskatchewan in 1800 all the way west into what would become Alberta, sometimes refers to it. Henry Kelsey in 1690 and Anthony Henday in 1754, both traveling for the British Hudson's Bay Company, came the farthest south of the North Saskatchewan River, but neither came as far as the south branch. Even Peter Fidler hadn't dipped down south of the Cypress Hills. But there were other reasons besides the lack of river systems for the lack of exploration.

I had thought the Cree and Blackfoot were enemies, but John Milloy in *The Plains Cree: Trade, Diplomacy and War, 1790 to 1870* cites evidence that there was a peaceful collaboration between them from about 1730 to about 1806 during which time they succeeded in driving south the Snake or Shoshoni people. After that there were short periods of truce, none of which lasted.

Peter Fidler's "Chesterfield House Journal," an account of the two winters (1800–02) he spent trading at the junction of the Red Deer and South Saskatchewan just north of the present-day town of Leader, about 175 kilometers northwest of Eastend, indicate no Cree presence, a friendly Blackfoot presence, and a danger so omnipresent from the Fall or Gros Ventre people that Fidler and his men abandoned their post in the spring of 1802, never having dared to go south of the Cypress Hills. According to Milloy, by circa 1850 the Gros Ventre had been pushed south of the Milk River into Montana too, and presumably were no longer a factor within the Palliser Triangle.

John Bennett of Washington University, in the 1960s, began a longitudinal socioeconomic study of the area centered on Maple Creek, which he calls "Jasper", a town seventy kilometers northwest of Eastend. In *Northern Plainsmen*, he offers what was the standard interpretation of the situation in the Cypress Hills area leading up to and just before the arrival of settlers:

> As this happened [as some of the Woodland Crees moved out onto the plains in search of furs for trading], a kind of no-man's land developed between the Plains Cree and the other tribes to the east and south; the Cypress Hills and the Jasper region were in the heart of this zone. The Blackfoot eventually dominated the area, maintaining garrisons in or near the Hills in order to keep other Indians from permanent habitation. The presence of grizzly bears in the Hills also discouraged Indian occupance. The Hudson's Bay Company more or less collaborated in this policy, since they were anxious to maintain the bison herds, to ensure the supply of bison meat (in the form of pemmican) for the posts, and to make profitable sales of guns and other articles to the Indians who did the hunting and trading.
>
> By the early part of the nineteenth century the situation had developed into a stable military frontier, with the Cree and their occasional allies, the Assiniboine, raiding the Blackfoot but generally fleeing before the implacable Blackfoot could retaliate in force. But the no-man's land policy held, and the long delay of white settlement of the region

was due to Blackfoot hostility and the collaborative desire of the Company to keep whites out.

John Palliser's accounts of his expeditions across the southern prairie from 1857 to 1859 bear this out. They reveal that although he was making plans to go farther south into the Cypress Hills proper, he was strongly advised by experienced members of his party that because of the Blackfoot whose territory it now was, it would be far too dangerous, and that if he persisted in his intentions, most of his party would desert him rather than go along. Palliser abandoned the idea and, except for a quick run on horseback down to the border and back on the Alberta side of the Hills by two of his men, Palliser and the rest of his party never saw the country south of the Hills either.

Between 1850 and 1865 the southern plains were relatively peaceful. But by the latter date the buffalo were disappearing and those remaining were retreating farther and farther to the west into Blackfoot lands. The Cree, desperate for their food supply, had no choice but to follow them into enemy territory. Milloy describes a party of Cree men in 1868 as having gone to the Cypress Hills, "one hundred and fifty miles inside Blackfoot territory," which would place the division of territory by the two nations at a line running north-south somewhere between Moose Jaw and Swift Current.

Many skirmishes and deaths were the result. A famous Cree leader, Maskepetoon, was killed by the Blackfoot during a battle in 1869 and this escalated the conflicts into a Blackfoot-Cree war all along the border between the two nations. Often their battles must have taken place in the very land where I live and walk, and that today is emptied of Native people.

In the fall of 1870 between six and eight hundred Cree and Assiniboine warriors — often the two nations are spoken of as if they were all Cree, since they often acted together, despite the fact that they spoke different languages — from all over what would become the province of Saskatchewan advanced all the way west through Blackfoot territory to the junction of the Oldman and St. Mary's rivers, near Lethbridge in pre-sent-day Alberta, where they were defeated in battle once and for all by the Blackfoot Confederacy. But by then there were almost no buffalo left in Cree territory — Bennett dates this as 1877 in the Cypress Hills area — and despite having defeated them, the Blackfoot began to allow the Cree to hunt in their lands. Thus, this territory where I live, once exclusively Blackfoot, became also Cree.

Fourteen years after Palliser's last Saskatchewan expedition, and two years after that decisive battle near Lethbridge, Isaac Cowie was sent to the extreme east end of the Cypress Hills — that is, in the Hills just outside of what is today the town of Eastend — to establish a fur-trading post for the Hudson's Bay Company. Today called Chimney Coulee, it had been a wintering place for the Métis, and doubtless before that for whatever Natives might have been passing through, hunting. Cowie was apparently the first European to come this far south, and he spent the winter there trading profitably with the Métis, Assiniboine and Cree, but not the Blackfoot, the very people the Company had hoped to lure into trade.

By spring he no longer felt it was safe to stay and he and a companion rode out from the post just ahead of a party of Blackfoot who shot the nine Assiniboine who had stayed behind to forage. The Blackfoot then burned the post to the ground. Isaac Cowie and his companion, Birston, heard the shots and saw the smoke from the burning buildings spiraling into the sky as they reached the plain below. Chimney Coulee is about ten miles from where I sit writing this, and from our northwest window I can see Anxiety Butte, the high point above it, on the ranch of a friend.

It was true then that southwest Saskatchewan had been the homeland of identifiable Native people, the evidence of which I saw everywhere I looked. All the more eerie and disturbing then to walk the streets of the towns and, except for Maple Creek, not see a Native face. And I still didn't know why. I decided it was time to look to the treaties.

There I found that the boundary of Treaty Number Four (1874), with the Cree and Saulteaux, or Ojibwa, included all of the area where I live, and also the Cypress Hills proper. Treaty Number Seven signed in 1877 with the Blackfoot, Blood, Piegan, Sarcee and Stony (Assiniboine) — the latter had to be negotiated with separately since they spoke a different language than the people of the Blackfoot Confederacy — describes its eastern boundary as "west of the Cypress Hills, or Treaty Number Four." Despite this, Olive Dickason, in her authoritative *Canada's First Nations: A History of Founding Peoples from the Earliest Times*, in her map of treaty boundaries, draws a dotted line around the highest part of the Hills, indicating that the boundary is uncertain. I thought that since this area was covered by treaties, there ought to be reserve lands designated within the area, and I spent some time trying but failing to find the papers which would show precisely where they were.

But then I found a paper by historian John Tobias called, ominously, "Canada's Subjugation of the Plains Cree, 1879–1885." In it I found a partial answer to the question why, after centuries of Natives living in and crossing this land, there is now only one small reserve of around three thousand acres, populated by about two hundred mostly Cree and some Assiniboine people, in the Cypress Hills area.

In a nutshell, when the buffalo disappeared in the late 1870s the Plains people were starving, and they massed together in the Cypress Hills area where there had always been game in the past, and where there was Fort Walsh, a North-West Mounted Police post, an agency of the government, and officials with whom to negotiate for land and from whom food, in the meantime, might be obtained. By this time more than half of the Native population of treaties Four and Six, chiefly Cree, was present in the Hills, a situation which alarmed both police and any other resident Europeans present. In 1876 Chief Sitting Bull of the Hunkpapa Sioux had crossed the border with four thousand followers immediately after the Battle of the Little Big Horn. Although it was a temporary situation, this move further alarmed authorities. With so many Native people massed together in one area, the possibility of an Indian confederacy and then an Indian war loomed large in their imaginations. (In fact, the leaders of the Cree nation,

Sitting Bull leading the Dakotas, and Crowfoot of the Blackfoot Confederacy did try to establish an alliance, but weren't able to come to an accord.)

For the most part, the Cree leaders had refused to take treaty, and the newly appointed Indian commissioner, Edgar Dewdney, saw in the starving people his chance to force them to do so. He ordered that rations be given only to those who had taken treaty. When the leaders then requested contiguous reserves in the Cypress Hills area, which would have resulted in nearly all of southwest Saskatchewan becoming Indian territory, Dewdney refused and ordered that all Native people must move out of the Cypress Hills area and onto reserves either to the east at Qu'Appelle or north of the South Saskatchewan River. Rations would be refused to anyone who remained. To ensure that no Natives would remain, in 1883 he ordered the closure of Fort Walsh so that there was no place in the area for Natives to obtain rations. Everyone, or nearly everyone, gave in, signed a treaty if they hadn't already, and left southwest Saskatchewan.

A small band under the leadership of Cree Chief Nekaneet remained behind in the Hills after the rest of their people had gone, living southeast of Maple Creek, presumably where the reserve is today. Neil John MacLeod, in an unpublished manuscript called "The Indian Agent," says that "they steadily refused to accept [benefits of treaty] and were a most independent people . . ." In 1913, according to the local history book, the local people signed a petition to the government requesting a reserve for these people, the result of which was a grant of 1,440 acres, which, in about 1940, was extended to include a further two and a half sections. It was not until the mid-seventies, the local history book says, that the group received — or accepted, depending on who tells the story — treaty rights. Their land became known as the Nekaneet reserve, after the one tenacious chief who had refused to be driven out. This ignominious and dishonorable history, all too commonplace as it is on both sides of the border with regard to the treatment of Native people by Europeans, came to a sort of conclusion in 1992 when the people of Nekaneet negotiated a land-claims agreement in which they at last gained the right and the funds to purchase a large tract of land in their beloved Cypress Hills.

I had learned that since the beginning of the seventeenth century and the first contact with Europeans who recorded what they saw, this area had been at one time or another under the sway of the Gros Ventre, the Blackfoot, the Cree and the Assiniboine, not to mention, in the most southwesterly corner, for a brief time, the Shoshoni. I'd learned that in the end, had it not been for the desperation of the people so that they signed treaties agreeing to leave the Cypress Hills area, my neighbors might have been Cree and/or Blackfoot; in fact, it is possible that these lands might never have been opened for settlement at all.

The little red sandstone scraper the writer and I had found in the grass had been made by someone; someone, whether Blackfoot or Cree, Assiniboine or Gros Ventre, or someone long before the existence of these nations, someone had chipped out that sharp edge and used it to scrape clean a buffalo or deer or rabbit skin. Holding the scraper in the palm of my hand, I tried to feel the presence of the other, a woman, I thought, who had used the tool. The way it matched the curve of my palm, the weight and balance of it so perfect for the work it was designed to do, its unexpected beauty, the unknown one who had used it, the mystery of the daily fabric of her life, drew me to it. Who was she? When had she lived? Who were her people? From where had they come?

Day after hot summer day I walked by myself in the dry, yellow grass, bent, looking down. Sometimes, coming upon a circle, I stooped and put my hands on two of the stones, feeling their coolness or their warmth. Someone had laid them just so — how long ago? A hundred years, when the buffalo were disappearing and the people were starving? On their way back from their fruitless search in Montana did they pause here and offer prayers to the four directions and lay these stones carefully, a modest tribute in all those miles of unmarked grass to say, *Here we stopped; here we offered prayers. Let everyone who passes know this was so.* Or perhaps the circles marked places where the powers of the land gave a good dreamer a dream, or a vision was granted someone. Or was it a thousand years ago? Or two thousand? Or nine thousand?

Stone markings in the grass; stone, the only available material, one that would withstand the summer fire and the winter sorrow; stone, formed when the earth was formed, older even than the ancient race who lifted it and made of it small homage to their gods. I pondered what I saw: the miles of yellow grass, the unimaginable depth of the sky, the unbroken solitude that was a constant possibility.

One day, as I wandered alone and on foot in a ten-section field, that is, a field of over six thousand acres, something strange happened. I had been driven out of the house by a jitteriness, an unnamed and inexplicable unease that prevented me from working or even from sitting still. As I wandered, instead of fading as was usually the case, the uncomfortable sense of need — but for what? — grew stronger. It seemed to me that I was out there for a purpose, that there was a place I was supposed to be, or that something was going to happen. I had no idea where or why or what, but the sensation was too strong to be ignored, or I had learned enough by then to know ignoring it as we have all been trained to do would be a kind of willful madness. I was free to follow it, free in time and in the circumstances of my life, and so I did.

I had no experience with whatever was happening to me any more than anyone else would have had. I bent all my efforts to follow this powerful sense of being drawn to something. Concentrating hard I realized that I had a sense that it was not my brain but my gut — my solar plexus area and my abdomen — that seemed best able to respond to this call.

I climbed a hill — I remember feeling puzzled and uncomfortable — looked around, and knew this wasn't what I was looking for. I went on another quarter mile or more and climbed another high ridge and looked around. But no, this wasn't the place either. When glaciers scraped down this countryside they left behind in some places scatterings of small rocks, in others none at all, and very occasionally a boulder called an erratic. These rocks, focal points in the landscape, had been used for centuries as buffalo rubbing stones and after the demise of the buffalo by cattle in a landscape otherwise bare of objects on which to scratch an itch or chase away insects. Somehow, I began to know that I was looking for one of these rocks.

I went farther down a ridge and saw a boulder in the distance, but I knew somehow that wasn't the right one. I saw another, but no, that wasn't it either. By this time in my life I was committed to the pursuit of these strange notions, even as I fully recognized them as peculiar. One part of me struggled to subdue doubt: what did I have to lose; maybe I was about to learn something that mattered about the world; I had spent too much of my life denying what I felt; I would not do that anymore. One part doubted, laughed at my foolishness; another part went on with certainty, serenely following what seemed to that part at least to be a genuine call from something other than myself.

I crossed another long, high ridge, started down the other side, and there it was — I knew it at once — the boulder I was looking for. I was suddenly afraid. I hesitated for a long time; more than once I turned away and took a few steps toward home. *Why am I doing this? There's something frightening out here. This is crazy. I'm going home.* I felt, there is no question about it, a force out there, and I felt it was acting on me to make me feel I had to go to that rock, and because I felt it, I was afraid. But I saw nothing unusual, heard nothing out of the ordinary. Each time I was about to start for home, instead I turned back to face the boulder again. *What are you afraid of? There's nothing out here to hurt you. You're imagining things.*

Finally I gathered up my courage and in a rush went down the hillside, across the draw and partway up the other hill straight to the boulder, feeling as though I were pushing away the air to get there, telling myself, For once in your life take a risk, be brave.

The rock was an especially beautiful one, a light beige blushing to pink in places, rubbed on its corners by cattle over the years to a smooth, mauve shine. I don't know what was important about it or why it was the right one and the others the wrong ones. I can only guess that it was meant — by whom or what? — as a marker so that I would find what I found next. After I'd studied the rock for a while, having exhausted its possibilities as far as I could tell, I began to walk the rest of the long flat ridge where I'd found it.

I began to find stone circles. There were about a dozen of these laid out in a long meander from the low end toward the highest point. Two of them were only half-circles; all but the half-circles seemed oriented toward the southwest. I walked along from the low end of the ridge where I found the first one, up toward the high end, finding them one after the other as I went, noticing the small cairns some of them had along the perimeters, the varying diameters of the circles. At the highest point there was nothing but grass.

I came to the smallest, not more than about six feet in diameter with a triple row of heavily lichen-covered rocks around the outside. I entered it — they all have what seem to be entranceways — and stood in the center looking, from my high position, out over the hills to the southwest. I felt a compulsion, a strong desire, to be closer to the earth. I knelt, but when kneeling only a small part of the body touches the earth, so I sat down, my legs stretched out in front of me. I felt — it was the same old story: part of me felt silly and part of me felt determined to do whatever seemed to need to be done — that something was happening; that some force was teaching me, that I should be still and quiet and listen, be alert for any instruction.

It seemed to me that some homage was required because I was privileged to be in such overwhelming beauty, and because I could feel that a power lives out there in Nature, some power for which I have no name, can't describe, don't understand. It was a primal moment and I gave myself, at last, over to it. I felt the natural thing to do would be to pay homage to each of the four directions, which I did, by simply facing each one quietly for a moment. That is all. After a time I left the hill and the field and went home.

I didn't know then that the four directions are a basic component of Plains people's tradition of worship. I didn't know that these stone circles were necessarily the remnants of spiritual ceremonies. I held myself still and obeyed what I felt guided to do. I have said that I have no Native blood that I know of and that I knew little about Native peoples' spiritual beliefs and ceremonies. Nonetheless, as a result of such experiences, I seem to have found myself drawn into their world as I seek to understand my own.

I am well aware of the discussions about cultural appropriation and about the gap between cultures and between the immediate experience of centuries of oppression and suffering endured by Native peoples of which I have no personal experience. (Although it is worth pointing out that the French side of my family has still not forgotten the expulsion of the Acadians in the 1750s by the English, when they were among the dispersed.)

I do not want to trespass; I do not want to make claims about or on things I have no right to and don't understand because my history is a different one from that of the Natives of the Great Plains. In fact, although I do believe in spirits and in local gods, I avoid theology, even in feminism. Rather than reconstructing or copying Native beliefs, these understandings of the spirit world, it seems to me, come with Nature, come out of Nature itself; come with the land and are taught by it.

In the course of my readings I had come across the assertion that the Cypress Hills area was regarded by Natives as sacred. When I first read this it sounded to me suspiciously like the romanticism of Europeans, and I paid little attention to it until I read the same statement, although unattributed to any source, by Dickason: "The Cypress Hills, near the international border where the Alberta/Saskatchewan border would eventually be drawn, was a sacred area for Amerindians, where hostile tribes could camp in peace." Isaac Cowie, in *The Company of Adventurers*, states unequivocally: "As far back as the memory and traditions of the Crees then living extended, these Cypress Hills . . . had been neutral ground between many warring tribes . . ." That this land was once sacred, in the light of my experiences, seemed more than plausible. When recently a fellow researcher told me that Stony (Assiniboine) elders in Alberta had told him emphatically that in their oral tradition this was so, I was hardly surprised.

In the intense summer heat, with mirages lifting fields beyond the horizon's edge into view in the sky, with grassy hill following after grassy hill, the one much like the other, and it much like the next, with the sky — immense, burning, infinite — swimming overhead and around one's shoulders, a man, a woman, felt free, or else felt she walked on God's lap, rested her head on his bosom, felt daily in the wind God's breath on her cheek, and in the burn of the sun God's fire, which might comfort or destroy. How else to live here, without going mad? And in the winter the icy, shining blue hills, the brilliant, dry cold inducing imagery of knives and cutting, bones and death.

Now when I looked out over the rolling hills and grassy plains I began to see, in the place of emptiness, presence; I began to see not only the visible landscape but the invisible one, a landscape in which history, unrecorded and unremembered as it is, had transmuted itself into an always present spiritual dimension.

KNOWING

When I decided to marry Peter and go to the country to live, I had expected to learn new things and meet new people; what I hadn't expected was to be changed myself in elemental ways by my new environment, not thinking that an environment in itself could change one in any essential way. I hadn't reckoned with the dimension that was the most basic ingredient of all in rural life: *that it took place in the midst of Nature*, that Nature permeated the lives of rural people, and that this was, more than anything else, the element which separated true rural people from urban people. I too would have to come to an accord with a life lived in Nature, and as I gradually began to do this over the years, that bottomless well of loneliness and sense of alienation that blighted my days would slowly dissipate. I'd been missing something from my understanding of the world and this new understanding involved more than other people and more than my intellect, but was also physical, somatic, an intermingling of place and person.

When I arrived I did not know what Nature was in its essence; I hadn't conceptualized it as having an essence. If, on the one hand, I knew in some sense we are all part of Nature, I also saw us — human beings — as essentially different from all the rest of Nature. I saw Nature merely as its effects, in a subject-object way. Of course, I knew about the dramatic and obvious effects on human life of Nature-as-object: crop-killing drought or hail, tornadoes that wrecked buildings, spring blizzards that killed the new calves, and lightning which split fenceposts, started prairie fires and killed horses and cattle.

I was aware and had no doubt about the reality of the less precisely described but fairly obvious effects of Nature on the psyche — the emotions, the heart — of spacious views, sunsets, sunrises, an unobstructed view of the moon and stars and their nightly turning, and the clear, fresh air, all of which I subsumed within a peaceful and beautiful environment, as most people do: Nature as background, as view, as landscape.

Thirdly, I had heard of the very subtle and rarely remarked on effects of a life lived in Nature, such as human relationships with wild animals or with places themselves — fields, hills, sloughs — or with fieldstones or gullies or trees. I knew that where these relationships developed, the method, the technique, the ways of developing them have no names, no delineation in scientific literature or existence in socially accepted ways of describing the world. They are sometimes called intuition, and the knowledge thus gained, or relationships thus established, I had placed in the realm of myth, in the true sense of the word. I did not completely discount them. I thought them either out of dreamtime, a time past, or belonging only to Aboriginal people still leading traditional lives; I had not considered such understanding of and through Nature — such relationships — as a possibility for anybody I knew, much less for myself.

These nontraditional relationships — with wild animals, with physical places — are probably not even universally present for rural people. For example, a few farm women don't go outside any more often than urban women tend to, and some very modern farmers use machinery so big as to have a Star Wars quality to it and requiring artificially controlled environments as in modern buildings, factors which act to separate the farmer from contact with Nature. How you view Nature is critical also:

as real estate, as resource, rather than as an extension of oneself, or oneself as an extension of it, as a larger creature with its own needs and desires and way of being in the universe. Whether or not and to what degree you accept Nature as she is makes a difference in whether you feel these effects or not.

I now to some degree comprehend these ways of knowing, but they were not obvious to me after a week, a year, or even five years of living in the country. I also think these relationships are so subtle as to be unnoticed by the majority of even those rural people who perhaps routinely experience them. Born as they are into the life, knowing no other, how might it become clear to them that they are experiencing things that urban people don't know about, that for the urban world these thing do not exist, don't happen, must be classified as madness or foolishness or romanticism? Since these things are just not talked about, it's hard to know who knows them in a conscious way and who doesn't, and I've come to believe something more than one's mere presence in a house in the midst of acres of uninhabited land is required before awareness will develop.

Occasionally in conversation it became clear to me how huge the gap is between an older person who'd lived all his/her life in the country and someone from the city: for example, it seemed incomprehensible, unbelievable to such people that one might live one's life never truly seeing the stars. Among such people these strange effects, although noticed, remain unarticulated, not a subject for conversation. And what we don't talk about, bring into existence by our articulation of it, remains deniable, is relegated to the realm of madness.

Because I was solitary and undergoing a profound spiritual crisis, I turned inward and became hyperaware of my own feelings, both somatic and psychic. Because I had lost my footing in the world and had begun to doubt I knew anything at all — that is, because I had lost all my self-assurance — I noticed them, accepted them for what they seemed to be. In a world that had stopped making sense I clung to my perceptions; I studied them; I felt these subtle forces acting on me. Feeling myself alone in Nature, turning to it as one might another person, I became sensitive to it in these mythical ways, ways I had little understanding of.

The last four years before I came to live in the country I spent working and studying in a large building with an artificial environment. Even though I walked back and forth to work most days and lived in a house with a yard rather than in an apartment building, I spent much less time out-of-doors than I do now, and when I was outside I almost never spent time in Nature in her natural state, but in city parks, or gardened backyards. I don't recall that I ever felt physically disrupted or out of sync with my physical self when I was at work during those years.

One spring I was invited to spend four days giving workshops and readings in Calgary high schools. I hadn't been inside such big buildings for any length of time in years, and I was surprised to discover how physically uncomfortable I was in them. Inside them I felt a disruption of my normal way of experiencing the external environment; I felt disconnected from my physical self. It was as if my body didn't end after all with the surface of my skin, and that some invisible, exterior part was being subtly disrupted by the machinery running the building. I felt as if I were minutely and imperceptibly vibrating with the machinery — I've felt this in airports too — as if I couldn't locate my *self* inside my body because the buildings (the furnaces, air-conditioning, fluorescent lights, removal from the natural world) were disrupting my normal way of functioning in the atmosphere. Leaving these buildings at the end of each day was a tremendous physical relief to me and I couldn't help but think about all the young people who were growing up mainly inside them, not even knowing that the buildings were warping, perhaps destroying, a dimension of their humanity. I hadn't realized to what degree I'd been physically changed by living beyond them.

For seventeen years now, every morning when Peter and I awake, after we have breakfasted, he, the rural man, goes outside to work regardless of the weather while I, held back by housework or the weather or work in my office, only occasionally go out immediately. Although I am deeply grateful for my modern plumbing, for my flush toilet, in a way I miss the many enforced daily trips I used to make outside, especially those in the middle of the night. They kept me in close contact with the natural world, the weather, the sun, moon and stars. I think I felt the natural world differently then than I do now when I choose when to go out and when to stay in.

I think of Aboriginal people whose entire lives were an interaction with Nature. It seems to me so clear as to be self-evident that living directly on the earth as Native people did, with constant, direct contact with the natural world, in tepees instead of on floors lifted off the earth by cement basements, would make different people of any of us.

A couple of years ago Peter and I traveled to New Mexico where we visited some of the dwellings of the Anasazi. At one site the local historical society had set up several kinds of homes constructed by the Aboriginal people of that area that the visitor might actually enter. One of these was a tepee and one consisted of a large, rectangular waist-deep excavation in the earth topped by a roof made of poles and brush and held up by stout posts. Around its perimeter were earth benches. I wondered how it would feel to live in such dwellings: sleeping in them, eating in them, entertaining in them, giving birth, being ill, dying in them.

It was late in the day and Peter and I had the place to ourselves. While Peter went his way, alone, I entered each of these dwellings. I tried to shut out any memory or sense of the house I had left behind and the motel I would soon be entering for the night. I tried to tune all my sense perceptors onto and into my physical self, I tried to *be* entirely in the moment, to feel only what I felt at that moment and to think myself into these places as my true and only home. It was a hard thing to do, but an act of the imagination which writers are supposed to be good at. I found I could maintain the full sense of this for only a moment, but that was enough to discover something.

I knew at once that my whole body felt different. I felt, not exactly heavier, but more substantial in a physical way; I felt more solid and the air around me seemed more real, more intense, more personal. Perhaps I should say that I felt more connected to the air, more connected to the earth, and that both of these were physical sensations which I felt with my whole body and were not merely psychic phenomena.

I can speak only of my own experiences in this regard, and I don't know if I'm unusual or not, although I really doubt it. I was making a conscious effort to note and examine how I felt, something which most people don't bother to do, but perhaps if more did — and had a range of experiences to compare — we might begin to delineate the parameters of such phenomena. I am not suggesting here that there is anything metaphysical about this sensitivity. This subtle but definite physical experience is a demonstration of a range of somatic perception — a way of knowing about the world — that I think urban living has dulled, if not destroyed.

But my life in Nature has somehow opened my psyche to other phenomena too. This effect I place in the realm of whatever it is that produces significant dreaming, and makes one become more intuitive — whatever intuition might be, but which as I've said I believe has to do with sensitivity to the natural world. The most puzzling and surprising occurrence in this psychic area (aside from dreaming) was this: I have mentioned how for a time books seemed to "jump off the shelf" at me. During the time this was happening, I always found the books that appeared to me in this way — books I had never even heard of, knew nothing about — were the very books I needed at that moment. As I mentioned earlier, *Journeys Out of the Body* appeared to me in that way, and although simple curiosity made me want to buy it, I thought that it would be self-serving nonsense and I shouldn't waste my money. I walked out of the store without it, only to return ten minutes later and, with some embarrassment and a lot of exasperation, buy it.

I took it into the mall and sat down on a bench to read it while I — like farm women everywhere — waited for Peter to return from his hunt for machinery parts. As I was walking out of the store with it in my hand, a strange feeling developed in my solar plexus which I classified as pain although it was more like a very strong cramp. I had no other symptoms:

no fever, no sweating or speeded-up heart rate, no nausea or bowel upset, just that strange, thoroughly uncomfortable, powerful cramp like a clenched fist in my solar plexus.

I sat down and began to read, but I had to keep changing my position in an effort to relieve it. No matter how I moved, sat up straight or slumped, twisted one way or the other, the cramp-pain wouldn't go away, though it didn't get any worse either. I was beginning to think about doctors and hospitals when I reached page twenty-one and read Robert Monroe's description of the same thing happening to him, the same gut-twisting cramp, the same bewildering lack of cause. My hair nearly stood on end.

In about twenty minutes the wrenching sensation went away. It repeated itself only once more about a month later as I lay in bed hovering in that state between wakefulness and sleep and, although this time it lasted only a few minutes, it was much stronger, and I wondered how Monroe could have stood it for the twelve hours he reported his had lasted.

I still don't know what it was, what caused it, why it occurred, what its purpose was, if it had a purpose, and it hasn't returned since. Monroe had no explanation either. He simply records that it "was the first out-of-the-ordinary event . . . that took place" before he began to do what he calls traveling out of his body. For the record, I have never thought of myself as having had an out-of-body experience. I mention this baffling experience, initially premonitory as it seems to have been, because it made me think that the solar plexus may be one of those places in our bodies aside from the sensory organs — visual, auditory, olfactory, gustatory, tactile — where a sensitivity to experience, to the world outside our bodies, may exist. The question is, what kind of experience? Is it only somatic, that is, a kind of extended somatic ability, or is it psychic, or a combination of both? Or was this merely an isolated, weird occurrence having nothing to do with anything else?

Earlier I described a peculiar feeling I had in my chest when I seemed to know something — the stone scraper my writer friend picked up — before I could have apprehended with my five senses what it was. I knew, too, that the object which I hadn't yet seen was something special; the way I knew it was by a kind of resonant, soundless thunk in my chest, which I perceived as a kind of slant-wise opening like a sudden shaft of light in darkness. From there the knowledge leaped to my brain and then was confirmed by my eyes. In the past in my novels and short stories, I occasionally described characters recognizing the significance of something by a kind of silent crash in their chests, and after the event above, I realized that I must have known about this way of knowing for a long time although it had remained below the conscious level.

In fact, the experience with the scraper made me think of the Bushman, Dabe, in *The Lost World of the Kalahari*, telling Laurens van der Post that the other Bushmen, miles back at their camp in the desert, would already know that Dabe and the other hunters had killed an eland. Dabe explained his people's ability to communicate over miles by comparing it to the white man's "wire", which he claimed Bushmen had in their chests. When van der Post and the hunters returned to camp that evening, they found that the waiting Bushmen did indeed already know, having made all the preparations for a big kill, which they would not have done otherwise. There was simply no way at all, miles away in that vast desert, for them to know about the kill of the eland.

It may be that what I felt in my chest was a remnant of a way of knowing that the Bushmen never lost and have developed so well that they can willfully use it to gain information as we use the telephone or the post office. It may be that if we take this possibility seriously and make the intense effort required, we might find again this way of knowing.

Not long ago, walking on the prairie, I nearly stepped on a large garter snake which raised its head as it coiled back from me, then stopped, waiting for me to attack or retreat. I felt a powerful sensation of combined shock, fear and something that might have been pleasure. The strange thing is that I felt all of that in my lower abdomen, in my womb, and it was a moment before I responded in the expected places: my intellect — "Oh, my God, a snake!" — my pulse speeding up, sweat breaking out on my body, and so on.

Even a day later when I was thinking about it, what I remembered was the surprising and powerful sensation in my lower abdomen, rather than how my heart pounded, or how I trembled, or screamed. In fact, I did none of these things, the abdominal sensation being sufficient until I got over my shock.

Penelope Shuttle and Peter Redgrove, in their fascinating study of the human female menstrual cycle and its implications, both mythic and actual, *The Wise Wound: Menstruation and Everywoman*, note that "the uterus is strongly supplied with consciously sensory nerves, but also with many filaments whose function is not clearly known to anatomy, as though these supplied an unconscious component — it is probable that all that the tissues of the body experience is in some manner accessible to our consciousness."

I believe that areas of the body other than the recognized five senses are able to apprehend information about the world which often is not available through the acknowledged senses. Although we North Americans for the most part don't, other cultures around the world believe in the existence and efficacy of one or another of these places, and make use of them as reliable gatherers of information, the Bushmen of the Kalahari as reported by van der Post being one of these groups. Stories abound too, for example, of the abilities of the holy men of India and Tibet to know things not available to the five accepted senses.

I begin to think that our technological prowess has outstripped, overwhelmed and in some cases destroyed abilities which we all once had, and which people who remain close to Nature have maintained. This would be of little consequence if technology were improving life and leading us on to greater things, but instead it destroys the natural world, and we thus lose a dimension of our humanity.

We are, after all, a part of Nature too. Why should we not be more capable of being tuned in to her than, in our urbanized, mechanized, indoor lives, we have memories of? If, put in a natural environment, being still and alert to new sensation, expecting only whatever happens and nothing more nor less, accepting such sensation as real and acting on it gives us new information about the world and/or extends our understanding of our place in creation, then it seems to me a practice worth pursuing. It may be that most people are so tense, so bombarded by other external stimuli and so disbelieving, such hard-core materialists, that they simply don't notice intuition when it does strike. It is possible that if we spent more time alone and in Nature our intuitive abilities — another way of gathering information about the world — would strengthen.

I walked every day. I was in a position few people, especially women, are ever fortunate enough to be in: alone, in no danger of meeting anyone, without a job or a boss, no small children to look after, no family, no pressing personal problems, no commitments and no plans. It was the first time since childhood I had experienced such freedom.

When I first began going out into Nature for my walks, I had been concentrating, usually for a fairly long period of time, and I had either grown too tired to think or I had run into a problem that I thought would be more easily solved after a break. My state of mind was nearly always reflective; I was usually sunk deep in myself, and I had trouble concentrating on just being in Nature.

On my return to the house I would sense that I had wasted my walk, since I'd been lost in thought the entire time.

One evening in early spring I was walking down a dusty, narrow country road between the river and a field of wild grass. I was alone and I had been walking a half hour or more when, for some reason I'm not aware of, I turned and looked back. I saw an animal hopping through the tall grass and I thought, Oh, kangaroo, and turned away again. Then it came to me that the animal couldn't possibly have been a kangaroo and I turned back to look at it, expecting it to be a fox or a coyote.

It was a four-legged animal, all right, leaping up on its hind legs in order to see over the high grass. It must have been a young animal because it was hopping with the delight of a child, playing, it seemed, although I knew, since it was sunset, it must have been on its way to the river to water. As I watched, it moved into shorter grass and then saw me, and it paused in its jumping and stared down the road at me as I stared up the road at it.

I was trying to identify it; the configuration of its ears and head was wrong for either fox or coyote; it was too big to be a fox; it moved the wrong way to be a coyote. I kept staring, waiting for it to change its position so that I could see I had simply been wrong and it was one or the other. But it didn't, and finally I realized I was staring at the first bobcat I'd ever seen in the flesh. And I think, given that it showed no sign of fear even when I clapped my hands, that it was staring at the first human being it had ever seen.

I had been in a reverie and for a moment when I saw the animal I didn't even know where I was, thinking that I was looking at a kangaroo here on the Great Plains. That is how far removed I often was from the world around me. Increasingly it seemed to me that if I was fortunate enough to have noticed certain things about the natural world out of my own unhappiness and consequent vulnerability, I had been given a gift, and I was throwing that gift away by not paying attention to my surroundings. I tried harder to pay attention.

Eventually I had done so much wandering that having gone in most directions many times, I couldn't decide which direction to go. When this happened — no direction looking more interesting to me than any other, no direction seeming to be the right one, although I've no idea what I meant by that — I would stop walking and simply stand there till I felt drawn in a certain direction. To do that I would concentrate, not on what was going on in my brain, which I tried actively to suppress, but instead on what I felt in my body, specifically, what I felt in my abdomen, especially in my solar plexus.

This practice led me to the first of my strange experiences on the prairie, the one where I first found the stone circles — where I felt drawn to them — and where I found myself trying in some simple and direct 'way to acknowledge the power I found out there. After such an experience, which felt to me complete in itself, I could not doubt the rightness of the approach, and I incorporated it into my daily walks. I began to tune in to this strange new perceptual experience which came from where I didn't know, and for which I had no name, and which required of me stillness, intense alertness and if not a casting away of the will, at least a subjugating of it to what I sometimes thought was a larger will.

I began to try to stop thinking about anything else but the dirt on the road, the grass beside it, the stones, the fields spreading out on each side, the hawks circling overhead, the song of the meadowlark or red-winged blackbird, the sound of the wind in the grass, a particular rock high on a hillside. This required concentration, I found, and a constant calling myself back from thoughts of other things to my surroundings at the moment.

I remembered something I'd read years before in Carlos Castaneda's *Tales of Power*. Don Juan had told Castaneda that he should learn to stop his "internal dialogue," stop the busy buzzing of the conscious mind with its flitting from subject to subject, stop the constant interior talking to oneself. Don Juan tried to explain to Castaneda that the internal dialogue is constantly shaping and reshaping the world for us, and that without it we would find ourselves in a different place, we would experience the world differently. To this end he gave Castaneda an exercise to do while he was walking. Castaneda, recalcitrant pupil that he was, found it a difficult task which he says he spent years trying to do and failing. But one day, walking alone down a city street, he suddenly found that he had inadvertently succeeded in stopping his internal dialogue.

It had never occurred to me that such a thing could be done, much less that it was desirable to do so, but out of the difficulty in maintaining concentration, I tried it, and to my surprise, not only could it be done, but I did it. Not for long, of course, only for a few seconds, and I noticed immediately that when I did it, I stopped breathing, which was a severe limitation on the length of time I could do it.

Inner stillness, which is what I was trying to produce, sounds like formal meditation. I had tried traditional meditation, strictly on my own without teaching or enrolling in a class of any kind, and had found it not only difficult but irritating in the extreme. I had used the classic approach: sitting quietly, alone in a room, my eyes closed, in absolute silence. I had concluded that it might be all very well for some people, but it was emphatically not suited to me. Yet at a writers' school one summer I suggested to the group that they might try "stopping their thoughts" as I had, in order to concentrate on a particular writing problem. I said I had tried but given up on meditation. Another writing instructor present who had had long, intense experience with meditation said to me afterward that he had laughed when I had said that I'd given up on meditation since my description of stopping my thoughts was in fact an excellent description of meditation.

Altered states of consciousness can have purposes other than gazing inward in a search for God. My reading on the subject increasingly leads me to believe that, for example, the best, the most successful of Aboriginal hunters are clearly in altered states of consciousness when they wait for and track game, and that this is brought on through intense concentration on the matter at hand and the exclusion of all irrelevant stimuli. Even the artist's moments of absolute absorption in his/her work take place, I believe, in an altered state of consciousness and are a kind of meditation. The same might be true of surgeons or cabinetmakers, fishermen, or children learning to read.

These strange experiences, although they'd happened one by one with long, uneventful periods in between, were beginning to seem to me to be parts of some whole which I'd never noticed before, or dreamt of, having to do with a way of understanding and being in the world. As a result of them I'd begun to approach the unbroken prairie in the way people approach a church or a great work of art — with a sense of awe and reverence at entering a powerful mystery. Once I had had one strange experience in it, how else might I have approached it, if I were to approach it at all? If wilderness has anything to teach us, it is about our own weakness, our failure to control much less understand this earth onto which we were all born. And with this growing humility in the face of the unknown, slowly a sense of being in the presence of some great consciousness, other than one's own, begins to grow too.

I became cautious. I thought, What if I am walking inside the mind of a creature — call it what you will — what if the earth really is a living being and my presence here is only on sufferance? If I am learning new things about myself and extrapolating from these things to this natural world and its nature, then it behooves me to walk carefully, to pay attention, to show my growing respect in every possible way.

I stopped picking wildflowers; I went around rocks instead of stepping on them; if I picked up a stone to study it, I put it back as nearly in the place and position I had found it as I possibly could. I did not glance at plants or lichens on rocks or on the ground, I studied them. I practised inner stillness in order to hear, really hear, the wind, the birdsong, whatever else might be in the air. It took tremendous effort and I failed more often than I succeeded, but I persisted out of a sense of discovery and of need. What is life? I asked myself. Why am I here? Or anywhere? What is the meaning of these stones, this grass, this landscape? I hoped that if I listened hard enough, looked hard enough, was still enough and quiet enough, the answers would seep into me.

One chilly, damp spring day as I was out on a rocky hillside by myself, I sat down on the wet grass and leaned back on my elbows, looking out over the landscape near me. Even in this desert country — if it isn't a really bad drought year when the hills look about to turn into hoodoos and there aren't many insects around — I have an impression of lushness, of many different kinds of grasses and shrubs growing against each other, resulting in a scene busy with so many different textures, patterns, colors, shades of colors.

I looked twenty feet away to a large patch of badger and rose bushes growing thickly in the cleft of a small coulee, a place where I knew deer often bedded down out of sight, and rabbits, when there are rabbits around. I shut off my internal dialogue for a minute (about all I can manage before I have to stop and start again), at which point all the sounds of the environment — birds, insects, wind in the grass or the sky — become clear. I was studying that copse with such intensity that something strange happened to me.

From my journal written not long after the *something* happened:

> *I was in the field to the north lying in the grass, trying to center myself again. I shut off my conscious brain activity — if only I could sustain that longer — and this time the sounds around me — I became aware of them, which I hadn't been before: insects, birds, chiefly the wind. But this time I had a sense of my "awareness" going out of me and not of these things entering me, but of me going out to mingle with them. Of being part of the sounds (which are Nature). Then I thought, this must be how the Aboriginal hunters did it, by mingling with Nature in this way and thus knowing where the animals are and what they are doing.*

This is a difficult experience to describe; after a few days had passed, I had to concentrate hard when thinking about it, to bring back its immediacy. I had recently read an article on such experiences by Pamela Colorado, an Oneida who had done her doctoral work at Harvard, who said that she was "just learning this myself," that is, "to have the ability to project yourself out," "to see what it's not possible to see." She goes on to say that "it is an ability that our people have known for thousands of years, and still practise." My experience suggested that this was true — both that some Native people could and can do it, and that one could learn to do it. Thinking about her remarks, I went out and tried to achieve it again.

And I succeeded, but for only a second, although it was long enough to convince me that it could be done. Some days later I tried again — some days I'm tired or upset or am not alone or conditions just don't feel right — and this time I thought I'd learned something new. I noted in my journal:

I didn't get a new sense — I shut off the ones I usually use and "clicked" into another kind, which I am sure is there all the time, but the others are omnipresent and obscure it. It isn't developing that sense that is necessary, it's learning to "click" that's required.

I have begun to think of this as "throwing" one's consciousness, though I don't feel at all confident that I have the necessary discipline to ever be able to do it beyond what I've already described. My speculation is that I don't *need* to do it, in the way that a hunter who depends on his skill for his food supply has a powerful need to do it, and that is why it is so hard for me. Or perhaps if I had learned it as a child, it would be easier.

And yet, it doesn't seem a useless skill to me; it seems a wonderful thing to be close enough to Nature to know Nature as Aboriginal hunters do. Who knows what the new, possibly even urban practitioners of such an art might learn about the world and how they might then change in their attitude toward Nature? More, in their attitude to life?

You have to be still and quiet for these things to happen; you have to release your expectations; you have to stop thinking you already know things, or know how to categorize them, or that the world has already been explained and you know those explanations. You know nothing. You understand nothing. You have only what your own body tells you and only your own experience from which to make judgments. You may have misunderstood; you may be wrong. Teach me, is what you should say, and, I am listening. Approach the world as a child seeing it for the first time. Remember wonder. In a word: humility. Then things come to you as they did not when you thought you knew.

I don't claim to have had a unique experience among non-Aboriginal people. I think of all the people I know who have lived on the land all their lives and those, fewer it's true, who have lived in such a way that they always had the desire and the time to simply sit and enjoy being in Nature. I think of Peter, to find an example close to home.

I think how, in the early days of our marriage when I was younger and before my knees gave out, we used to spend whole days on horseback checking cattle. Often on a hot summer afternoon we would sit on the grass high on a hillside, while our horses grazed beside us, drowsing in the sun while we waited for the cattle to water before we moved them home or to the next field. It was a new experience for me, and I always found something magical in it; it seemed so extraordinary that one might spend a life full of moments of such peace, purity and serenity.

Indeed Peter had spent his life like this, day after day on horseback, herding cattle or checking them, in all kinds of weather. Knowing this about him, how at ease he is on the prairie, completely at home, how familiar he is with the habits of the cattle, horses and wild animals of the plains, with the grasses and the wind, I thought that just possibly he might have experienced this throwing of the consciousness as I had, almost involuntarily. Because it wasn't in his vocabulary, and there was nobody around to tell anyway, and quite possibly if it did happen, it wouldn't seem strange to someone of his experiences, he'd hardly noticed it and had never mentioned it. I asked him, and he said, deeply embarrassed (we had company at the time), with characteristic taciturnity, that he didn't know. What he meant was, I think, this is not something to talk about.

I leave him his secrets. But who knows what the old farmer who never married and never modernized, who spent his life out in a weatherbeaten shack in the midst of a sea of grassy hills, or the devoted gardener, or even the occasional birdwatcher or ecologist might have experienced much to his/her surprise, when there was nobody around? And if someone like me says it out loud, will more people admit to having had it happen to them? And then more people try it, thereby changing themselves and, ultimately, the world?

If I had left behind a lot — a career, family, friends, an established round of life — and gone into what seemed a void, where I had begun, I thought irrevocably, to sink into its black depths, slowly a whole new light was dawning, and I was beginning to feel as Christopher Columbus must have when he first saw the shores of the New World: tremendous excitement, joy and relief. And this must also have included, for Columbus as it did for me, a measure of chagrin to discover it was already populated by people who took for granted and understood what for us was a world of immeasurable treasure and wonder.

ANIMAL KIN

One autumn not long ago, visiting at the northern cabin owned by one of my sisters and her husband, I was stunned by the blaze of gold, orange and red with which the bush glowed as if it were imbued with its own light, making it appear fragile and buoyant. I had not remembered this. All my childhood memories were of gloom and menace, the heavily scented darkness of the earth, the terrible, soul-stirring cries of the wolves, the bears lurking everywhere. I grew up with a fear of wild animals that was of a very deep and primeval kind, kin to that of cave dwellers defenseless against marauding animals.

My earliest memories as a child are of bears: early one morning, my father standing on the step in his pajamas, clapping his hands loudly over his head so that two bears who are snuffling through our clearing pause, look up and quickly shamble off into the woods; our mother, alone in the night with us small children, putting the lit kerosene lamp on the window ledge instead of the table, explaining that she does this so that any approaching bears will not see their reflections in the glass and try to get into the house. In the north, bears — interesting, charming — whatever else they might be, are always first to be feared.

I remember also from that time sitting at dusk on a swing in the school-yard in a tiny village set against the bush. Timber wolves begin to howl not far away in the forest, and I move so that I'm sitting with my back to them, while shivers run up and down my spine.

When I came here to live, a particular pleasure was the constant presence and sightings of wild animals, most often of small herds of antelope, especially if they crossed the prairie in front of the truck and I got a close look at their power and their amazing bursts of speed. It seemed wonderful to get up in the early morning and look out the window to see a pheasant strolling across the grass, a brace of grouse pecking in the garden, a pair of deer feeding under the window or seven coyotes strolling across the field on the other side of the yard. It was like living in your own private zoo.

Since I thought I'd found a landscape where there were no animals one needed to be afraid of, when I saw antelope, deer, coyotes, they weren't much more to me than interesting and beautiful cardboard cutouts. Peter's horses and cattle were presences more real, but at the same time, I thought riding a horse would be like driving a car, and that the cattle would offer no resistance to a rancher's plans for them. The nature of animals was only one more aspect of rural life about which I had a lot to learn. That it is an aspect at the absolute core of it, I also had to learn.

Although as children we kept housecats for pets, and I remembered how our mother's father talked lovingly to his team of big workhorses as if they were people, I had no experience of animals that felt personal to me, and no very great feeling for them.

When Peter and I were first married he had a herd of three dozen American Saddler horses, including a stallion. I watched him, often working with his friends, breaking horses, trimming their feet, doctoring them, even castrating them. They did not hurt animals. They did what they had to do and, for the most part, enjoyed their work. As I watched I began gradually to see their deep respect for animals, their admiration of them, their nearness to the ones they knew well and yet, despite their calm acceptance of them, the eternal distance that remained between them.

A favorite entertainment when there were visitors was to chase the herd in. What fun that was, hanging on for dear life in the back of the half-ton as it bounced wildly over the prairie, and how thrilling to watch the herd streaming across the fields and up the alley to the big corral. Then Peter would put part of the herd into a smaller corral, cut out a few to bridle and saddle or, when we still had colts, cut the new colts out so that the visitors could pat them and talk to them to gentle them. Then Peter would begin to teach them to lead.

But of course on a working ranch when it was time to change saddle horses in order to give those in the corral a rest and to keep those in the fields in riding condition, Peter would chase the herd in on horseback. Then he would cut out the horses he wanted to ride, turn out the ones he had in, and eventually let the herd go back out into the fields. Usually he kept them in for a few hours, though, so they would remember they weren't wild horses, and feed them a little and let them find the electric stock waterer so they'd know where to get water during times when the sloughs and dugouts were frozen or had dried up.

For the first while I was very afraid of the herd racing around in the corral. I stayed on the other side of the fence while Peter walked among them, choosing the ones he wanted, one at a time, raising his arms, stepping in front of them as they ran, calling to them, then murmuring softly to the one he had managed to stop as he put a halter on it. I saw how they went around him, no matter how fast they were running, how they seemed to be carefully trying not to hurt him, although they might easily have run him down and killed him.

Obviously it wouldn't do for a rancher's wife to be afraid of horses. But it is one thing to be helped up onto a saddle horse in a corral where there is only one other horse, also saddled, and to stand in the middle of the churning dust as several dozen horses, many of them never broken, race around within inches of you.

On one of these occasions when Peter had chased the horses in and left them to stand in the corral, I went out with him to open the gate to let them go back to the fields. We were alone, our visitors having long since left. It was evening and the sun would soon be setting. Peter went into the corral while I lingered on the other side. "Aren't you coming with me?" he asked. The horses were standing quietly in the evening stillness. A nighthawk whooped softly, huskily, as it swooped low to sit on the fence at the other end of the big corral. A horse switched his tail at a fly. Nothing else moved, even the perpetual prairie wind had died. I allowed myself to be coaxed into the corral.

We walked slowly from the gate into the center and stood looking from horse to horse. Peter talked about them: about selling this one or that, about breaking this one or that one next, about the origin of a scar on a mare's flank. A kind of peaceful hush had settled over the corral. We stood till we grew tired and then walked a few feet more to sit in a relaxed silence on the edge of an empty feedtrough.

We sat a long time together with the horses. Once or twice one of Peter's saddle horses strolled over and put his nose down to us. We didn't move and he wandered quietly away again. As we sat there a kind of enchanted mood descended over us and over the corral, as if the two of us were, for that little time, a part of whatever the horses were, caught in the same spell, till the sun descended below the horizon and it was almost dark. Then we opened the gate and waited while the horses slowly moved out into the pasture.

After that, I was no longer afraid to go into the corral with the herd, and although I was cautious, eventually I helped him cut out the ones he wanted from the herd of racing animals. This mightily impressed my sisters when they visited, although nobody else around here would be fooled about my courage or know-how.

One day Peter and I were out riding and were waiting for the cattle to go to water before we chased them into the next pasture. We sat on a hillside holding our saddle horses' reins as they grazed beside us. We waited a long time, more than an hour. Peter even dozed off, while the cattle moved almost imperceptibly toward the waterhole. I was getting bored. Peter awoke and sat up.

He was riding his usual horse, a big bay gelding, a horse nobody else ever rode. Now the horse moved close to Peter, lifted a front hoof and gently brushed Peter's thigh several times. I froze, caught in a mixture of surprise and fear; Peter laughed. "He wants to go," he said.

I had never thought that a horse might have an opinion, that it would occur to him that he might be allowed an opinion or a desire as pets are, or that he thought at all. He weighed about twelve hundred pounds, and seemed to me to have no way to communicate, yet he had stroked Peter's leg gently, aware of his power, but careful not to hurt him. From that moment on my attitude toward semi-domesticated animals like this one began to change. I became less afraid and more curious about them, and also more accepting of them as fellow creatures with innate natures of their own.

As I was beginning to get closer to domesticated and half-wild animals and becoming more enlightened about them, I was also beginning to have encounters with wild animals. These were often less benign, but they nevertheless served to increase my curiosity about them, not curiosity of a casual kind so much as a growing sense of a deep mystery that needed solving before it would be possible to live easily in this landscape.

One day I stood across the river on a high bank picking chokecherries while on the other, lower side a white-tailed doe, unaware she was being watched, fed at a tree and talked steadily to her fawn. The sound was somewhere between a whinny and a whistle. I had never heard it before and never have since. I find myself anthropomorphizing her, imagining she was teaching the fawn the lore of the prairie, or more likely as a human mother would do, using her voice to keep the fawn content and nearby. But maybe she was vocalizing for the sake of vocalizing, or for all I know, she might have been having a conversation with the tree.

Occasionally when we were out riding, a coyote would follow us for hours, sometimes getting very close to us, pausing every once in a while to call. I was pretty nervous when they came very close, although Peter, for whom this was unremarkable, was entirely unafraid. He assured me that there had never been a case on record of coyotes attacking a human.

On my daily walks I liked to go far enough out to be out of sight of power poles and lines, buildings, fences, any sign of human occupancy. In a place where there were no longer any bears — the Cypress Hills had once been full of grizzlies — or any wolves or swift foxes, I never seriously thought there might be any reason not to. But one day as I was strolling along more than a mile north of the ranch house, the cattle dog I had taken for company suddenly abandoned me and raced toward a hill ahead of us and to the right.

I saw a coyote running the line of the hill on an angle slightly toward us and to the east. I was not afraid, partly because I was used to them following us when we were on horseback, and also because "coyotes never attack humans." I called the dog back. When he came to me, I turned, intending to head back closer to the house. Then I caught a glimpse of something moving behind me, also on an angle toward me, but some distance back. I froze and waited. It was a second coyote, and in that instant, in a flash of understanding, I saw that two coyotes were circling me as they would prey.

Terror swept through me. I ran; I ran as fast as a non-athletic forty-year-old could. I was out of breath in what seemed only a moment, and when I stopped to catch my breath, my lungs wheezing painfully, and looked around, the landscape looked exactly the same. It looked to me as if I had been running on the spot. I was mystified. The pain in my lungs signified that I had run a very long way and yet I appeared to have gone barely any distance toward the house, although it's true that one grassy hill looks a lot like another. In any case, when I thought to clap my hands together over my head as I'd once seen my father do so many years before, the coyote closest to me — I think about fifty feet and still running toward me — paused, I swear cast me a disgusted look, then veered off. I didn't see where the second one went.

Besides the puzzling perception that I had not run any distance, there was also the circumstance of the weather. Peter and I had just returned from a two-week holiday driving from the northwest corner of British

Columbia to the southeast corner. It was late fall, but it had been ninety degrees Fahrenheit for three or four days in a row, and this was so strange at this time of the year that the prairie had taken on an otherworldly aspect; there was a tension in the air; I felt that something was about to happen, something out of the ordinary; I was waiting for it.

Here I was being circled as prey by a pair of hunting coyotes, one of which seemed to stare hard at me, and then rejected me as if finding me not worth the trouble. I was not only terrified, I was chagrined. If it is true that no coyote has ever attacked a human, and I believe it is, then what did they want? I couldn't help but feel that this might have been the opportunity I'd been waiting for to actually communicate in some direct way with a wild animal, that if I'd not been such a coward and had stood my ground, something enlightening might have happened.

Because I had originally believed I was in a benign landscape, I had forgotten my childhood fears of wild animals until my encounter with the pair of hunting coyotes. I began to see that even if there are no life-threatening animals in this landscape, there are excellent reasons to keep a good distance between yourself and relatively harmless ones. One of my first encounters, with a badger, which backed up against a rock, rose on its hind legs, and in a most threatening manner appeared to swell, extended its claws and hissed ferociously at me, taught me that here was another animal from which I'd be wise to keep my distance. I startled a porcupine once, and it's putting it mildly to say it startled me. The porcupine, about a foot and a half from my leg, in a move that I liken to the sudden flipping of a venetian blind from closed to open, flashed from fur to a shield of quills and froze that way. I gave an involuntary shriek that sounded like a deep note from an organ and that hurt my chest, while my scalp crinkled. I couldn't get out of there fast enough. And then there are snakes, which I'd just as soon not mess with either, even though in this pocket of country they are all harmless.

There was so much about rural life I hadn't understood. With regard to animals, it seemed more and more amazing to me that every empty field, every hillside, every unplowed road allowance or stone pile or patch of tall grass contained wild animals. That animals had a kingdom in, around, beside ours where they lived out their lives and went about their animal ways, fitting into Nature — being Nature — in a way humans can't seem to. I knew that already grizzlies, wolves, swift foxes among others, all native to the area, had been completely eliminated, and that burrowing owls were threatened and now ferruginous hawks too. I had a sense that there were people who wouldn't care in the least, would perhaps even be glad, if all the wild animals were destroyed. I wondered what would happen to the landscape if that were to occur. Would anything happen? Would it matter? Why would it matter? When occasionally someone made a derogatory comment about animals, I kept silent, but I kept watching and pondering questions like these.

If we find wild animals interesting, it sometimes also works the other way around. Early last spring Peter came up to the house to say there was a coyote hanging around the corrals; why didn't I come down and have a look? It was only 6:30 in the morning, but I dressed and valiantly went down to see it. In the big corral the yearling cattle were standing crowded together in a semicircle staring in silent wonder at a thick-coated, grayish white coyote who stood quietly in front of them, seemingly paying them no attention.

Peter had the camera, and I stood a few feet back of him as he took pictures, getting as close as six feet from the animal. The dog got as close as he dared, which was closer than Peter or I, sniffing, then moved back to stay with us. The coyote didn't run away or make any move to threaten us. Sadly, he had mange, a kind which affected only his hind quarters and tail, which hadn't a hair left on it. Peter snapped a few pictures, we talked about the coyote, his condition, wondering what he wanted, and after a while I went back to the house and Peter went back to feeding cows and the coyote trotted off, disappearing behind a windbreak. When we thought to look again for him, he was gone.

He was back the next morning. I stood in the living room watching him as he rolled and chewed some bones the dog had abandoned, then went to the row of cars and trucks and circled each of them with an edgy trot, stopping for a quick sniff, then on to the next, circling back, zigzagging, stopping, moving on. He was in the yard every day that week. He and the dog arrived at a standoff, one going down to feed on the fresh carcass of a dead calf down by the barn while the other waited by the house, then trading places. Once the dog went too close to him, and from the window I saw the coyote show his teeth. In an instant he went from a delicately built, harmless-looking creature to a ferocious wild animal — he seemed suddenly all teeth — and back again.

Peter said that in his fifty and more years of ranching he had never seen a coyote behave in such a way. How did he know we wouldn't hurt him? Was it because in all the years we've been here we've never hunted anything? Have cheerfully fed skunks and raccoons and magpies, creatures other people shoot, from the food we put out each day for the barn cats and as a snack for the dog? I like to think that's so, because, after all, in every corral that time of the year, every year, there's the fresh meat of cattle that didn't make it through the winter, and always some of the coyotes we spot have mange, but despite this, no coyote had ever come to live in the yard here.

The following week, returning from a walk down a little-used country trail, I found his corpse lying peacefully on the grass by the side of the road. Someone passing by and seeing the coyote's condition, which would ultimately have killed him, had shot him as he was about to cross the road.

Even though that person was right — the coyote would soon have died a miserable death from mange — I was filled with dismay. It seemed to me that he had come in out of the wild propelled by the same curiosity about humans that humans have when they try to get close to wild things, and I treasured his presence, felt there was something magical about his having come to us. I mourned that little coyote to an extent that surprised even me. His sudden death left me with a sense of a gap, an abrupt truncation of an experience that promised to yield more. And I could not reconcile myself to that casual, unthinking shot.

Although Peter doesn't hunt, many of our neighbors do, sometimes for a taste of wild meat, sometimes for trophies or to sell the fur, and sometimes — probably most often — to eliminate what they feel are pests. More than once I have been amazed and then offended to hear people remark that there are too many deer, coyotes or foxes this year and that people ought to go out and kill a bunch of them.

It isn't that I don't understand the impulse: the day the two coyotes circled me, I was afraid. If I'd been used to it and had had a gun, I suppose I might have tried to kill at least one of them. When raccoons in the yard eat all the dog and cat food set out in the yard, a gun is one solution to the problem, and if during calving season there are a lot of coyotes around, it only makes sense to think about protecting the calves. But I had always been one of those city people who hate hunting, believing, although knowing nothing about it, that non-Native hunters were gun-crazy and cruel and filled with nothing else but a lust for blood. I couldn't imagine that urge as anything else but perversion. Now that I was living with animals every day and giving serious thought to their place in our world, I began to examine more carefully my set of beliefs with regard to them, and to wonder about hunting them.

Hunting out of necessity, for one's food supply, is a different story from shooting animals as pests or hunting when one could more easily buy the meat at the supermarket. And there are different ways of hunting out of necessity. For example, the respect Native hunters show for their prey is legendary, stemming as it does from a different belief system than ours. Hugh Brody, in *Maps and Dreams*, tells of accompanying Beaver hunters who had killed and were butchering a cow moose:

> As always, virtually every part of the animal was taken: the digestive system was cleaned out, the intestines separated from other entrails, the liver and heart carefully set aside. . . . They observed also the conventions that surround the treatment of an unborn calf. First, they prepared a thick bed of partially

digested browse which they poured from the animal's stomach. . . . Each part of the surrounding reproductive system was disconnected from the womb and set aside. Then the womb itself was placed on the bed of the cow's stomach contents and sliced open . . . the foetus was carefully laid on the mat of stomach contents, protected with more digested grasses and some membranes, then covered over with spruce boughs and a few dead branches. Such respectful treatment of the foetus was as automatic as any other part of the butchering . . . there was no question of its not being carried out.

If there is to be hunting for food by non-Natives on any large scale, this kind of respect for animals needs to be learned, or rather relearned. The origins of hunting as a human activity are so old that they are lost in the past — there are, of course, still some hunting cultures extant today — but because of its very age as a human activity, it appears that to eat other animals is instinctive and subdued only by an act of will. One of the greatest transitions for most of the human race took place ten thousand years ago when farming was invented and survival strictly by hunting gradually became, in much of the world, a thing of the past. The chief reason for this act of will seems to be a spiritual one: the belief that it is wrong to kill and eat other animals.

But hunting to live, facing starvation otherwise, engenders in humans a very powerful respect for the animals which must be killed, while hunting for sport, precisely because it isn't necessary, can engender a casualness, a carelessness and a lack of respect for the animals. To the extent that we kill casually without good reason, we brutalize ourselves, we brutalize the human race.

John Haines, the American poet of excellent reputation, off and on during his more than twenty-five years in the Alaska wilderness made his living by running a trapline. To be both a poet and a trapper is a strange and contradictory combination of professions, the one requiring unusual sensitivity and thoughtfulness, the other unusual coldness, possibily even cruelty, or at least the ability to shut off feelings. His book *The Stars, the Snow, the Fire: Twenty-Five Years in the Alaska Wilderness* addresses the dilemma of hunting: what harm, in the true balance of things, someone killing animals for their fur actually does, and what the true nature of animals themselves is, questions that are at root intertwined. Haines acknowledges the sense of mastery that the hunter feels:

> There is passion in the hand that pulls the pelt and strokes the fur, confident that it knows as second nature all the hinges and recesses of the animal body.

But he acknowledges that he was haunted by the animals he trapped.

> I lay awake at night, watching my trail in the snow overhead, and saw myself caught in a trap or snare, slowly freezing to death. I felt the cold grip of the metal, the frost in my bones. A pair of great yellow eyes seemed to stare at me from the darkness, and looked into my soul. Very likely I bestowed on the creatures more capacity for pain and suffering than they possess, but there was no way to be sure of this. Their lives and deaths haunted me like a wound in my own flesh.

In the end even Haines the poet, the contemplative and educated man, cannot quite resolve the dilemma, nor feel quite at ease with himself. For him, the mystery remains, both of the true nature of the animal and thus of whether he did wrong in doing something which so satisfied him.

> But however close that familiarity, something is always withheld; the life of the animal remains other and beyond, never completely yielding all that it is.

Like Haines, I don't understand the why of them; I don't know what their essence is, or what they know of existence and death, or of the meaning of their own lives. At their core, they remain strangers, as Barry Lopez says, the Other. What is that "all" that Haines speaks of which even the intimate knowledge of joints, sinews, organs and blood never reveals?

Those who study animal behavior in its natural setting and who make films of the naturalists' work for programs like "Nature" and "The Nature of Things" seem to me to be merely trying to fill up the void between us and them with interesting but not very useful facts, facts which give the illusion of understanding. Ask a question and they have an answer to give; it will not tell us the thing we most want to know, that we all want to know. And it often seems to me, watching scenes of animals in the wild copulating or killing each other, that despite their reverential tones, attempts either fumbling or whimsical at explanations of behaviors that don't make sense in terms of human understanding, and in some cases their clear anthropomorphizing of them, in their unbecoming inquisitiveness, nobody shows less respect for animals than the people who make these films.

If we do not come to truly know animals as trappers, hunters, naturalists, zoo-goers, photographers or pet owners, the question of how we might come to answer the essential questions about them remains. North American Natives are, as always when Nature is invoked, instructive on this point. Faced with the necessity of hunting them to survive, and thus being forced to know their habits and behaviors as well as or better than professional naturalists, they dealt with the mystery in two ways: one, they treated them with reverence as Hugh Brody describes and as is reiterated many times in their own words and in quotations and descriptions gathered by anthropologists, explorers, traders and missionaries, and in their carvings and paintings; and two, because they played such a large part in their lives and their dreams, they believed on another level they were at least emissaries of the gods, sometimes embodiments of them, and tales sprang up to explain creation in terms of them.

Peter Knudtson and David Suzuki in *Wisdom of the Elders* quote a statement made by an Inuit hunter named Ivaluardjuk — Joseph Campbell also quotes him in *Primitive Mythology* — as it was reported by Arctic explorer Knud Rasmussen:

> The greatest peril of life lies in the fact that human food consists entirely of souls. All the creatures that we have to kill and eat, all those that we have to strike down and destroy to make clothes for ourselves, have souls, like we have, souls that do not perish with the body, and which must therefore be propitiated lest they should revenge themselves on us for taking away their bodies.

In the hierarchy of being of some Native mythologies wild animals are placed closer to the gods than are humans. This is a view that accepts and honors the fact that in our fascination with science, we in the modern world have forgotten and denied the ancient and continuing mystery at the core of the animal, the mystery at the heart of Nature about which Haines has written so eloquently. The longer I live out here, the more I think that that Native belief must be true.

As the years passed, I found myself more in tune with the animal world around me. Walking in the hills one day, over an area I often walk, I came upon the skull of a yearling deer. Although the animal had been dead long enough that the skull was white, it had not been there a few days before, and I drew the usual conclusion that a coyote had dragged it there. It didn't occur to me to wonder why a coyote would have bothered since any trace of flesh or marrow had vanished, and there were no teethmarks where an animal had gnawed the bone for the calcium.

It was a beautiful skull: bleached to a pristine whiteness, small, delicate, with slender antlers swelling outward, then curving gracefully inward to point to each other in perfect symmetry. I picked it up to look more closely, thinking I had never seen anything before of such grace, such pure loveliness. I held it in both hands, gazing down at it, and as I admired it, I turned to face in the opposite direction. As I turned, I glanced up and there, standing evenly spaced along a higher ridge, staring quietly down at me were twenty-two mule deer.

The moment was, as Aldo Leopold says of the beauty of a flight of cranes, "as yet beyond the reach of words." I felt blessed in having found so perfect a skull; when I turned and saw the deer hovering over me, watching me as I picked it up and admired it, holding it with reverence, as if it were somehow holy, it seemed to me as if they had given me the skull, as if it were a gift to me. In fact, as I told the story months later to a group of artist-conservationists in South Dakota, one of them said spontaneously, in an awe-filled whisper, "Ahhh — it was a gift." At moments like that, rare as they are, I feel that every sacrifice, every second of pain that has been the direct result of coming here to live has been worth it and more. Here I feel myself constantly moving close to a level of understanding about the nature of existence that I can't imagine coming in any other way, in any other place.

In the evening, during the night, and in the early morning coyotes sing to us from out on the prairie. They are actually calling to their brothers and sisters across the valley or from hill to lonely hill. Sometimes they sound happy, yipping delightedly out of sync with each other, without melody or decorum; other times their song seems a heartfelt lament to the gods, as humans sing of their sorrow, their suffering across the centuries and around the world. When they start their song, we never fail to stop and listen to them.

Of all animals of the plains, coyotes have the greatest sense of humor. Live with them for a while and it becomes evident why in Native theologies, Coyote is the Trickster god. When they are singing as they sit on the hillside in a more playful mood, it's easy to think they are laughing. Watch them taunting a ranch dog, or taunting you, and you know they love nothing better than a practical joke.

One day a coyote and I fought a match for the possession of our dog, and I think I won in the end, only because I kept moving closer and closer to civilization. The dog and I were strolling across the prairie, when suddenly some distance away a coyote appeared. As soon as he saw the dog he called to him from a low hill. The dog responded by turning and running toward him. I whistled to the dog to come back to me. The dog turned and started back; immediately the coyote called again and kept calling till the dog turned back and started toward him. I kept walking in the general direction of home, and the coyote, getting a little closer, moved from hill to hill behind me. He would call the dog, the dog would start to trot toward him, I would whistle and call the dog by name, he would begin to return, whereupon the coyote would come a little closer and call in a most compelling, urgent way till the dog turned again to him.

Even when I finally reached the road and had called the dog back to me again, the coyote found a hill with a clear view all the way to the house and sat there doing his best to lure the dog back. Or maybe he was singing of the enchantment of freedom, of the wild life, a memory of which stirred in the dog's bones with each note of Coyote's song.

It seemed plain to me that even though he was trying his best, the coyote didn't really expect to win, and that was why this was all a big joke. Nonetheless, with the whistling and shouting and trying to get out of there as fast as possible, I was exhausted, and annoyed besides. I wanted to scold that coyote: it's not funny! Smarten up!

When I reached the road and looked back at him on the last hill, I yelled, "Get a job!" to the coyote. His response was a particularly joyful, contemptuous riff before he turned tail, and looking back over his shoulder as Coyote does and always has, he headed home to his den. A half-mile down the road I looked back again. Coyote had paused to sit on the highest hill, silhouetted against the sky, to yodel one more time, no longer at me or my dog, but to the sky, or to nobody and nothing in particular, to the universe, a signature cry, saying *I am*.

Of all the interesting, strange and beautiful things I have seen and felt living here in the landscape, none have stirred and puzzled me more than my encounters with animals. I say "puzzled" for want of a better word: these encounters have struck a chord as deep as life itself, have opened up a darkness inside me resonant with knowledge that chooses to shape itself as questions rather than answers. After any one of these encounters with wild animals, feeling I had for a split second glimpsed the creation of my long-ago vision of universal oneness, I had to find a way to express this. I would write, and that knowledge I had almost grasped I tried to formulate as the light that would illuminate my characters, my story. However I might fail or succeed as a writer, I would not have been one at all if I had not come into the landscape to live.

Natives — from what I know of their traditional lives from "as-told-to" writings — have no difficulty accepting that dreamworld is as real as the flesh-and-blood world of every day. I am unable to do that unequivocally. I still cling to this everyday world, out of fear, out of the apparent loneliness and lack of human warmth in that world, out of uncertainty that it is right in the sense of morally defensible to accept wholly the dreamworld. That is how it is that, seeing a coyote in flesh and blood I am afraid, or see him as Other more than I see him as a fellow creature with whom I might possibly communicate, despite the fact that in a breathtaking dream a coyote looked meaningfully at me and I wasn't afraid.

For example, once I came upon a crescent of stones half-buried in the grass and almost completely covered by lichens, both circumstances suggesting, but not completely proving, that they had been placed there in very ancient times. The crescent was about seven feet from point to point, and I immediately thought of the moon and of lunar worship. That night I dreamt that I was to establish a place of worship for women at that site. This I certainly did not do; I thought, If I were Native, I would follow the dream's instructions, but I am not Native, and the very idea of even suggesting such a thing to women makes me feel like an utter fool.

Despite my awe, my sense of blessedness, my overwhelming gratitude for these visions and dreams, in practical ways, most of the time, I carefully hold the two worlds apart.

And yet sometimes it seems to me, this last year or so, that when I see a coyote watching me, or deer near me in a field, I am less afraid or startled than I used to be. Sometimes I even think that they are less afraid of or startled by me, as we both hold still and from a safe distance study each other.

LUNA

I had been here seven years when my sense of alienation and being alone
in the world had culminated in the dream where I saw the word "anomie"
written across the sky. Thus began a period lasting about five years of the
most intense psychic travails. I have read and reread my journals in an
attempt to sort out the important things that were happening in my personal life — my mother's cancer and eventual death, a severe illness of
Peter's — what was going on in my writing life — the publication of three
more books — my psychic journey as it was expressed in dreams, and my
extensive reading in order to understand what was happening to me. I feel
like Psyche who was taken by Venus to a huge pile of many grains mixed
together — wheat, barley, millet, vetches, beans, lentils — and ordered to
sort them into separate piles before nightfall if she was ever to regain her
happiness. Psyche despaired. But while she was given help by a hill of ants
who did the job for her, I seem to be on my own and will never be able to
make a perfect separation. It probably doesn't matter if it isn't perfect;
what matters is that I feel reasonably satisfied by the way in which, after
diligent effort, I have managed to sort my experiences of those years.

While Psyche's reward was to be reunited with her lover, Cupid, things are not so easy for mortals. We are never free of trials, but they do become more understandable and therefore more bearable as one grows older.

I seem to have spent 1984 gearing up for what was to follow: the period of mysterious dreaming which was at its most intense in 1985, and especially 1986. Sometimes the dreams were simple and symbolic, but more often there was a narrative thread to them. Night after night I crossed the Saskatchewan River on foot, alone, in the dry summer heat with the sun beating down and the shore the palest sand; sometimes I crossed by a bridge on which I could never reach the far side without putting my life in danger; sometimes I waded across. I was always carrying snakes, passing snakes, being harassed by snakes, some of which were clearly magical in that they were often a shade of red — from coral to wine — and glowed as if with internal light. Night after night I was in water, sometimes the river, more often the ocean.

As I look through my journals it now seems to me that what seemed at the time to be separate dreams were sometimes increasingly detailed and more profound versions of the same dream. For example, in November 1984 I had the first of three dreams in which I was in very deep water on a raft. In the first dream the raft was crossing Halifax harbor and I was swimming beside it holding on to a rope. In the second, in March 1986, the raft was a brilliant pink, a magical color, and it was growing smaller and sinking so that I was sometimes up to my neck in great waves, although the raft never completely sank. The third dream, about five months after the second, was extensive, detailed and deeply disturbing, and this raft had a captain. She was a woman.

In fact, I had many dreams about women, mysterious dreams, often in which two or three of my real-life women friends would appear together as my companions, once in which my sisters and female cousins and nieces appeared as all the same age, a flock of beautiful young women, wearing white dresses, who ran together laughing. In the two most important of these dreams a strange, powerful woman appeared and was the central figure. And finally, in early 1987, this series seemed to culminate in a dream in which a dwarf woman, another magical figure, appeared and with the brightest and most welcoming of faces, invited me into her home. The major dreams of this period haunted me and I spent literally years with my nose buried in books trying to understand them.

At the beginning of 1985 before I had finished *The Gates of the Sun*, I had already begun to think about my next novel, which I had decided would be about the women of this farming/ranching community. I had already begun to call it *Luna*. It becomes very difficult to set these events in a strict chronological order, but it would have been about the same time that I tackled Robert Graves's magnificent, spellbinding and eccentric masterpiece, *The White Goddess*.

The older I get and the more I see of the world, the more I understand the extent of, and the more sorrowful I feel about, the subjugation of my gender: about how men abuse women, the best men, with the best motives, by completely missing the point, by failing to support even in trivial ways, by expecting us all to be mothers to them whether we are or not, in short, in small ways, day after day, century after century, denying us our full humanity. Robert Graves, whatever he might have been in his personal life, did women a great service when he wrote *The White Goddess*. Reading it was like opening a door in a shabby house into a room filled with treasure. That it might be possible to believe in a feminine universe! That women might be whole! That we might have a history of our own, an archetypal existence not as wounded, failed men, as graceful handmaidens or chattel, but as *women* were or *woman* was, at the deepest level, amazing and gratifying to me. I never wanted that book to end, but when it did I set off in search of other books of comparable depth, vision and sensitivity toward the feminine.

It helped of course that I was thinking hard about *Luna* and how to write it. Through a mixture of my own struggles to find a workable Self, my dreams, and my sense that I couldn't write a book about women till I had a sense of who women were — who they had started out as at the dawn of creation, who they were aside from the warping of the patriarchal culture — I began to read books about women by women, since both Jung and Freud had failed me in this regard. While most of the many books I read were by women, I didn't shun books simply because they were written by men. Early on I sought out Esther Harding's *Women's Mysteries*, but I also read Erich Neumann's *The Great Mother*. I began to read female Jungian analysts, especially Marion Woodman *(Addiction to Perfection* and *The Pregnant Virgin)*, and Shuttle and Redgrove's *The Wise Wound* and, later, Redgrove's *The Black Goddess*. I read Adrienne Rich's *Of Woman Born*, believing that a poet could tell me more than a feminist academic. I went back in time with the books of feminist archaeologists like Marija Gimbutas who wrote *The Language of the Goddess*, among others. I read the books of feminist theologians, historians and more eccentric writers like the woman who calls herself Starhawk. I read myths in which women appeared, believing that if there was no record in history of who we were thousands of years ago, perhaps the truth was lodged in these ancient stories and I might tease it out and piece it together. I tried to figure out what was basic and universal and to separate from it what was not. (It is basic and universal that we give birth to children.) I was trying to find a grounding in the feminine both for myself and my own life, and for the women of my book *Luna*. Where I was not driven by the needs of my book, my dreams drove me.

In April 1985 when I had been thinking about *Luna* for a few months, I had one of the major dreams of my life. In it, I was trying to cross a border into a foreign country which was a desert country, very hot and with palm trees everywhere. My companion was a woman. Both of us were wearing white robes and headdresses which were like both those nuns wear and those of desert people. Our headdresses fit tightly around our faces, hiding our hair, but hers had a black band on it which mine didn't have. I seemed to be her acolyte. As we approached the border guard he spoke to her in another language. She said to me in an undertone, "You'd better think of an Arab name," but I couldn't. The name I came up with was that of a

Jewish friend, but I was able to cross anyway because then I was sitting high on a hill at a round table under a tree with my companion and two or three other shadowy Arab-looking figures, I don't know if men or women, but who seemed to be smirking at me. In the center of the table was a bowl of fruit. In a casual, unthinking way I reached out, took an orange and without peeling it, bit into it. The woman told me that I should have washed it first, that it would make me very sick, that I would die. She then pointed to the bottom of the hill where I could see through the palm trees small rectangular buildings which she said were houses for washing fruit.

What was most extraordinary in the dream was the woman herself: she was authority itself, but at the same time she was completely without emotions. I don't remember her voice, but she had smooth, light olive skin, a full face and dark eyes. When she spoke it was the absolute, unadorned and unequivocal truth, conveyed without a hint or trace of affect — no pity, no anger, no affection or warmth or coldness either. She had to be a representation of an otherworldly figure, and I have always thought of her as such, as a goddess, or as Jung might describe her, as the Wise Woman, or as other less imaginative people might, as a wiser aspect of my self.

She appeared again three months later in a dream, but this time she was robed in a gown like the white one — black this time — but that resonated richly with hints of other colors. Her message, which she conveyed twice while looking straight into my eyes, was a hopeful one. Twice, with absolutely no hint of eroticism, she showed me her breast, a symbolic gesture saying, I thought, that life was still full of sustaining richness and beauty.

The dream about eating the orange is still clear and bright in my memory. I puzzled over it for years, searching book after book for clues as to what it meant. In fact, I didn't fully understand it until I was writing this book when I suddenly realized that a paragraph I had just written — a metaphorical statement of the problem in my coming here to live — was, in fact, a statement of the dream: how I had closed my eyes and leaped and when I opened them I found myself in a strange country, with strange customs, where I didn't even speak the language. I had always known that the dream had to do with death and I had made the common mistake of wondering if it was a prediction of real death. I began at last to see that it was about the death of the old Self, the Self I had been when I first took that major step of giving up my old life and coming here to make a new life. That I had not known what I was doing when I reached out for the fruit of this life, and that as the dream said, it had indeed killed me. Even the symbolic orange which so baffled me I finally realized was the fruit I associated with wilderness — on my first visit here I had been stricken with déjà vu when I was offered an orange.

In mid-July 1986 I dreamt I opened a book a friend had given me and inside it I found an old, pressed twig. As I watched, the twig grew full and round, its leaves unfolded and swelled and turned green and it became a branch. Then, one by one, three trumpet-shaped, blue flowers sprang out on it and blossomed to fullness. I awoke and thought of Aaron's magical rod that brought plagues to the Egyptians, of the golden branch hung with bells the Irish poets — ollaves — carried with them in honor of Brigit, Goddess of Poets, of the Golden Bough which Aeneas plucked from a tree and carried into the underworld, which made it possible for him to return to the upper world (and which both Frazer and Graves remark was mistletoe), of Gilgamesh who, with great hardship, went down to the bottom of the cosmic sea to collect the Branch of Immortal Life. I thought of the ancient and recurring symbol of the Tree of Life.

I searched through my books for an interpretation on a level more clearly a part of my daily life and found this in Jung's *Man and His Symbols*: "An ancient tree or plant represents symbolically the growth and development of psychic life [as distinct from instinctual life commonly symbolized by animals]." I took this as a sign that I was nearing the edge of the forest, that whatever I had been through in my crisis was resolving itself, that I had survived these trials and that things would begin to be easier, clearer, simpler, although I could not see how, nor any reason why they should.

I have mentioned a deeply disturbing dream in which the ferry captain was a woman. It occurred on August 15, 1986, which is — in view of my intense efforts to find some grounding as a woman, both for myself and for other women, I am sure not a coincidence — the night of the Assumption of the Blessed Virgin Mary, and in pre-Christian times, of the chief celebration of Diana, the Moon Goddess. It was the night of the day I finished the first draft of *Luna*, ten years after I had come here to live, and this dream, too, is as clear to me now as if I had dreamt it only last night.

It was the third of the raft dreams and in it I was swimming in inconceivably deep water alongside a barge, which I hung on to with one arm. The barge was oily and dark and loaded with boxes. It had only one passenger, a Victorian gentleman wearing an overcoat, a hat, a scarf and gloves. His face was completely hidden and only his dark eyes glowed out at me. The captain standing at the wheel was a woman. She was tall, slender, with long, thick, wavy honey-blonde hair. She wore a captain's hat, a heavy dark jacket, a narrow short skirt and her feet and legs were bare, a detail which seemed in the dream to be very important.

It seemed to be night, although not so dark that we couldn't see, and we were crossing a deep, dark river. I was swimming as hard as I could and finding it difficult, kicking and thrashing about and swimming a crawl stroke with one arm while I held on to the barge with the other, but I had no sense of giving up. Far, far below me in the depths of the water, I could see faintly a gigantic man-o'-war. We came to a house and the captain stopped the ferry and I wandered through the house, while she opened and closed all the cupboard doors searching for something. In the bathroom she looked at her reflection in the mirror. The house had no curtains and no furnishings at all, and there was no glass in the windows and no doors in the openings and the floor was unimaginably deep water. Then we were at a second house. It was exactly like the first, except that it had a damp mud floor. Again she searched it. I thought, But how will the ferry get through here? And I felt such a sense of an adventure

156

abruptly cut off, of a voyage ended too soon. The dream ended without the ferry reappearing, with me stuck high and dry in the empty house.

That dream also took me years to decipher. Eventually I realized it was at least a version of the myth of Persephone. We were crossing the River Styx, a river of the underworld which the dead had to cross, ferried in myths by Charon, a male, who had to be paid a coin. (Apparently the Greeks used to leave a coin in the mouth of the dead person to pay this fare). My ferry captain was a love goddess, a goddess of the moon, both of which were revealed by her very beautiful long hair, her bare feet and legs — which are sexual symbols on one level, and on another, quite possibly a substitute for a mermaid's tail — and the mirror into which she looked. The passenger was hardest of all to determine, but in the end I finally realized with a shock of understanding that he was Hades, whose name means "the unseen" (hence his numinous invisibility), the lord of the underworld who married Persephone after stealing her away from her mother, Demeter the Corn Goddess. This is, of course, one level of interpretation, called the "night sea journey." Another level would be to say it was a dream about my life crisis, my search for a happy and fulfilling life.

Then I realized that I had received the magical bough a month before I made my dream-journey into the underworld, and on the mythical level, the gift of the flowering bough was what made it possible for me to go there and to come back again safely.

Around this time I had also begun to dream about girl children, babies and little girls who were so charming and interesting that I gave up celebrations to be with them, that I followed them down dark, rainy streets in the night. One of these little girls wore a siwash, a heavy sweater which is knitted by Native women and decorated with symbols out of Native mythology like the sacred Thunderbird.

On the August night of the most ancient celebration of female goddesses, I had dreamt the dream that symbolized what I had been through, and in which I sometimes think I met the goddess for the first time. Six months later I had another of these "culminating" or "summarizing" dreams in which the Wise Woman appeared to me again near the end of the dream which had taken me from the flock of beautiful, laughing young women to a meeting with the first man I'd ever loved at eighteen — and we were both young again — through numerous horrors, including being attacked by a red knight on a red horse, who lowered his lance and charged me so that I stepped behind a leafless, dead-looking, stark bush which saved me, to her welcoming face offering me peace and solitude in her clean, bright, serene abode. And, truth to tell, I seemed more afraid of what she offered me than of even the red knight, for I said quickly and spontaneously, "Oh, no! I'm not ready yet!" and the dream ended.

It has taken me another seven years to understand the flow of these dreams and to see them finally as expressions on a symbolic and some-times archetypal level, of the progress of the life of my woman's soul from girlhood into a measure of maturity and understanding. It has taken me all these years to clearly understand the nature of the crisis I underwent, believing as I did that it was solely about my move here into the country and the loss of intimate companionship and my independent and fun-filled (although also filled with travails) way of life.

In fact, the numinous figure of the dwarf woman, who looked rather like my first mother-in-law, a truly wonderful woman, and whose apartment looked like my mother's house, was a figure representing maturity. I believe she was offering me the emotional peace and wisdom of old age. She was telling me, Your youth is over, this is what is left, and I refused it, as most of us do. It is hard to leave behind the passions of youth, the unremitting hope and the constant sense that a great and marvelous adventure waits just around the corner. I was not ready then, seven years ago.

I feel that I ought to acknowledge the woman-goddess in these dreams, but like so much else about them, I am not sure what to say. I have read enough books by feminist authors to know that a good many women have taken such a figure with great seriousness and are now fol-lowers of the Goddess, in the same way that others are Christians or Hindus. I resist taking this figure so literally, and as I reject all forms of organized religion, and detest theology, I can hardly join a new church, no matter what I might think or do in privacy, no matter that it might at last celebrate womanhood.

I've attended exactly one feminist ritual, rather by accident when I happened to be in Toronto on Hallowe'en and a friend invited me. What was most satisfying about it, I thought, was to be with women who, with a mutual sense of awe and pride and humility, were accepting and celebrating their womanhood. At this gathering one of the women present told us about another, larger gathering she had attended where one woman couldn't stop giggling as the group went about its rituals, till the leader grabbed her by the shoulders and shook her: *"Do it right!"* she demanded, through clenched teeth. It's a small step, I thought, but it ends in the Inquisition. Let us, in our newfound understanding, pride and strength, not repeat the errors of men.

And yet, there *is* a feminine soul which for centuries has been kept in chains, prettied up and trotted out on special occasions where it is dutifully admired, condescended to and then dismissed, never allowed to blossom into its full, breathtaking beauty and power. It has been twisted and warped, resulting in horrors like cosmetic surgery and anorexia, and the idiocy of the cult of youth. Even today in most places in the world women are, at best, second-class citizens and, at worst, slaves. I believe without a shred of doubt in the existence of this soul, and I believe, too, that there is an archetypal feminine soul, existing in that mythical world, the world of dreamtime, which we reach at last in dreams and waking visions and which informs our lives as women every day. This, I believe, is what we must tap in to; this is what we must keep our hearts and our souls tuned to, for it is the truth as nothing else is.

This personal crisis, this major dreaming, these books I read culminated on a more practical level in the writing of *Luna*. I had begun thinking about this book late in 1984 and finished the final draft in April 1987. It was first published in the spring of 1988 and fell out of print fairly quickly, where it remained till this year. Of all my books, to this day, it is the one I am most often asked about by people — ninety percent women — who have read it or who want to read it.

When I began *Luna* I might have, at that juncture, gone back to the book about women I'd tried to write seven or so years earlier whose protagonist was an urban career woman, but I didn't. Instead I chose to write about rural women, about women who led traditional lives, because I thought that the themes I was dealing with would be easier to find and elaborate on in lives which were still close to those women had been leading for several thousand years: giving birth to children and nurturing them into adulthood, the growing and preparation of food for the family, making the family's clothing, being homemakers, women who lived inside the home and marriage, without outside careers, in an enterprise — the farm or ranch — which was necessarily jointly undertaken by all family members.

Much of this life is lived out-of-doors, in the garden, on horseback, in half-tons driving across or parked in wheat or hayfields or pastures, and at social events which are much more often held out-of-doors in the country than in the city. As I've said, in rural life the sense of Nature all around one is an integral part of the life, as is the constant study of sky and weather, fields and hills. And the rhythm of Nature becomes part of one: the endless cycle of Nature, the rising and setting of the sun each day, the monthly lunar cycle, the seasons, the births and deaths and rebirths, as seen in farm animals, in wild animals, in gardens and fields. A rural woman can feel so much more strongly herself as a part of Nature than a woman in the city can because Nature's example is all around her, and her rhythm is the rhythm of the feminine.

The women of *Luna* are, like me, trying to understand the meaning — the size, shape and boundaries — of their lives as women. They are struggling to delineate the place that motherhood has or should have in their lives, not merely as women, but as persons, as human souls in the universe. So I began with the idea of a female creator and all that that might entail, and by delving into prehistory and mythology, I structured the book so that it is a re-creation in modern form of the Greek Mysteries.

I found so much in the traditional life that was and is beautiful, where the nurturing role of the feminine is allowed to flower fully, where in a city it cannot as easily because of the dispersal of energy inherent in city life, because of the impossibility of raising a family on one working-class income so that the woman has to hold down a job outside the home too, and because most people have no little plot of land to grow things for their own use. I had decided *Luna* would be about modern-day women who still lived a traditional life, but I was also thinking about my own life and my own struggle to find a fulfilling and appropriate way to live and, also, my mind was full of the lives of my mother, my grandmothers, my aunts and my sisters and female cousins.

I thought about my friends in the city and their struggles to juggle home and family and career, and of the general destructiveness and pain of divorces which were so commonplace there, of the whole generation of children being raised in poverty and with only one parent. It began to seem clear to me that if women had gained in personal freedom and self-determination by abandoning or being forced off the land, for one reason or another, and out of that traditional life, they had lost some valuable things too, the chief one being a stable support system in which to raise their children in peace and security, a terrible loss from which society, I believe, has not yet begun to feel the full and awful effects.

Nonetheless, if the traditional life had been so right for women, then why did so many of those who still lived it often hope for something better for their daughters? Certainly the traditional life had its bad side: subservience in women and their denial of it, abuse of women's dependence by men, who sometimes turned their wives into something close to slaves, and who used them as objects on which to take out their frustrations and rage. Less often, where formal power is denied women, the rare one will use the power inherent in her femininity to keep the children submissive and the husband frustrated in his masculinity. Far more often, though, the situation is one of men merely taking for granted the woman's complete and self-denying dedication to him, the children and the farm. It is out of situations like these, I think, and the incessant round of work, that women dream of better things for their daughters.

Though our mother was never subservient, nor our father domineering, I tried to think more specifically what was missing from my mother's life, most of which she had lived in the traditional way, from raising chickens and a huge garden to making our clothes, from little overalls to run around in when we were little to our high school graduation dresses. She worked too hard and never had enough time for the books she loved; she had more children than she wanted, although she did not ever want to lose one of the children she had. She wanted to have more education than she had been able to acquire as a young woman during the Depression and she wanted more art and music and theater in her life, a little more glamor, a little more ease. More to the point, I don't think she would disagree when I say that she had a dream of a different life wherein she might find more fulfillment for herself as a person, an individual. None of these are evil things to want; they are not even unreasonable. And all of these are themes among the women of that generation in Saskatchewan.

Even while I deeply admired the women around me, I doubted that I would be happy in that traditional life which while it had a certain clear nobility to it, also had too much potential for making a virtue out of the inherent possibility of martyrdom, a way of life for women and an attitude for which I have no admiration at all. And it seemed plain it wouldn't give me the opportunity to try out all my gifts, all the things which I thought I had it in me to be or, at least, that I wanted to try out, whether I failed or I succeeded. For many of us life is bigger than the round of gardening and diapering and cooking that takes up so much of the life of a traditional woman. Womanhood is bigger even than that; I want a part of the bigger life, as it seems men have.

What I didn't realize then was that I wasn't the only one struggling to make a life for myself in a world which was so abundantly fulfilling to the men but, no matter how much they loved their families and rural life, in a lot of largely unacknowledged ways was stifling to many of the women. Women, too, have intellects, and intrinsic in the human brain is a vital, lively and unkillable curiosity, an absolute need for new and interesting sights, sounds, ideas, a need for challenges and for intellectual growth. We were geographically very isolated: we couldn't take university classes whether for credit or not; we couldn't go to art galleries, lectures, concerts, plays, even movies were hard to get to; if we had professions, other than teaching or nursing, they couldn't be pursued without moving to town or city; we couldn't keep up with fashions or extend and deepen our knowledge of the vibrant, exciting world of urban women, which, whether we fully approved or not, meant being able to take an equal role in sports, politics, business and the professions.

We did not all feel completely fulfilled by helping with the traditionally male work of seeding or combining, or swathing hay or baling it, or cutting out or chasing cows, but did it because we felt it our duty and because we wanted to see our husbands happy and the enterprise succeed. (I couldn't help but notice that if it was our duty to help with the men's work, the men were rarely seen in the kitchen helping can vegetables or diapering the baby or sewing the daughter's graduation dress.) And the rural, traditional life means that women work all day long for the sake of other people — people they love, it's true, and whose happiness is their happiness — and have to steal any time for themselves for activities not a part of homemaking. Because genuinely free time is in such short supply, there isn't time for an individual woman to search out and learn about what would be a fully satisfying activity for her, if it were possible to find such activities within her geographic range. Besides the problem of time, there is the problem of discretionary income. On a ranch or farm any discretionary income — of which there is less and less these days — tends to be turned back into the business, for new machinery, more land, farm buildings or livestock, to pay the omnipresent debt, or given to the children so they can go to the city for more education, or to start them on their own places.

A few years ago at a dance, in the context of a conversation I no longer remember, I remarked to the table of couples Peter and I were sitting with, "This life is great for men, but it's killing for women." There was dead silence around the table, I never knew if because of embarrassment at my speaking aloud a taboo sentiment or, as I thought, more likely because every couple at the table had had long, anguished, and ultimately unresolvable conversations in the dark of night about that very subject. Indeed, what man would give up his farm or his ranch and a life he loved merely because his wife was less than fulfilled? But it was many years before this fact came home to me as closer to universal rather than as merely my own problem, at least in this sense of women needing personally fulfilling activities, and a little more variety and stimulation in daily life.

As I read and wrote and dreamt, it began to seem clear to me that all our women's lives in this century were false to the extent that we had only one model for life and it was the one devised by males for us, and that we were lost and twisted and at sea and would not find our own strength, the rightness of our lives, and the beauty of our womanliness until we found out who, in our deepest female essence, we are. Now the story of Persephone began to seem to me to be a story about not only my life but lives of all women, stolen away from girlhood and our mother's protection into the world of men, of Eros, never to be persons in our own right. I thought that if women are often petty and small-minded on occasion and bicker endlessly with one another in ways less characteristic of men, it might be because we have no dignity in our womanhood and never say to ourselves, I am a woman, as men say, I am a man, to remind themselves of the nobility and courage this image requires of them. I did not think our subjugation would end until each of us was able to say from the depth of her soul, I am a woman, meaning, I am half the universe, I am made in the image of the goddess, as men at least for the last five thousand years have been saying, I am made in the image of God.

Women experience the world differently than men do. Experiencing it differently, we know different things about it than they do, we experience *life* differently, and if left alone to try it, we would live it differently. And as a writer I thought, We haven't yet told our stories out of the fullness and uniqueness of our femininity. We haven't yet told the truth about our lives. Until we tell the truth out loud, no matter how humiliating or painful or at variance with society's version, we will not come to know what we are, what is truly our world of experience, and through that, what our roles should be, what we can be.

That was one result of my long sojourn in the metaphorical wilderness — I began to believe I had to write out of that deep, abandoned, forgotten, ignored and discredited place in myself where surely I would find what there was in me that was wholly woman. I thought, The only way to find out what a woman is and might be is to speak only the truth out of one's own feelings. I had been tending toward what is dismissively referred to by scholars as "confessional" writing as it was. Now I thought, I am a writer; why else would I write except to express how *I* experience the world? I wanted to cut away what I had been taught, I wanted to shut my eyes and close my ears and my door and only write from the deepest part of myself, to say how things seem to me, what I honestly think about my life and the lives of women, or further, what I honestly *feel* before thought, about the world and my experience in it. I would use the material around me, but I would see it with my own eyes, hear it with my own ears, sense it with my own body.

Because I was writing a novel about women's lives, one of the issues I examined with seriousness was why it was I felt I could not have friendships of the kind I'd had in the city with women in the country. What was it I had talked about with my old friends that I couldn't find anybody to talk with in the same way here? The conversations with my city friends, for one thing, had a high degree of intimacy even in friendships of very short duration, acquaintanceships really, which here, as nearly as I can tell, seem to take years to build. That was one difference. The other was subject matter. My city friends and I had talked about feelings, more than anything, I think. With great subtlety, shades, nuances, of feeling and emotion were dissected and laid bare. All this to a degree that my country friends would regard as obsessive and peculiar, perhaps going too far, going beyond the limits of good taste where privacy is concerned on the one hand, and on the other, approaching triviality, even wasting time when there is work to be done.

Perhaps there is no more to it than that — beyond, of course, the unavoidable fact that all my urban friends were part of the university environment where talk is highly valued as the means of exploring ideas and developing them, where one might display one's wit and articulateness to mutual joy, where talk is an art form. But while urban academic people believe anything can be said, and would be better for it, rural people tend to take the opposite view, feeling much is better left unsaid, and that judicious silence has, on occasion, a greater eloquence, is the greater good. Even on "coffee row," where talk is, as they say, cheap, this style of conversing prevails.

I am a writer; I am a thinker, and sometimes a talker. Nothing seems full and real to me until I have either talked about it or, as is most often the case, written it out, crossed it out, written it again and again and again till it makes sense to me. I will always go too far, say too much, examine nuances too minutely for everyday life. Also, I see now that my expectations were wrong in the first place; those old tête-à-têtes came out of a different way of life, different expectations and experiences, a different fabric of day-to-day life. Thirdly, those virtually obsessive conversations were, I think, all of us, each of us, working out our own destinies in the way available to us in such a milieu. That was how we did it, but it is not how country women do it.

I inhabit another world now, where all of this is worked out physically, in canning and sewing and driving the combine, where sorrow and rage and bewilderment are worked out in sky and hills, grass and wind, in the song of the meadowlark and the nightly cries of the coyotes, in the mystery of the northern lights and the moon and stars.

As the years had passed it had become increasingly clear to me that I could not live a life like the women around me no matter how much beauty I found in it. Peter didn't expect me to, I had no children at home to care for, and it seemed foolish and empty to live the form of the life without the content — canning and pickling for nobody, changing sheets twice a week and ironing them for somebody who couldn't care less about that sort of thing, and I cared nothing for it myself, staying home every day in an empty house. Understanding that and then accepting it in a final way took a long time, the understanding of it the longest.

Once I faced that, and that I could not erase my past, everything that I had been, everything that I knew, my personal history, the next step simply came clear to me one day as I stood looking out the northwest window toward the distant butte that marked the place where the history of the town of Eastend began. The women here are right: I *am* different from those who were born here and grew up here and lived their lives here. It is no use at all to try to be like them; it is time I stopped trying, stopped even thinking about trying. It is time I accepted my life for what it has been, time that I accepted myself for what I am.

From that moment on everything grew easier. I no longer made any effort to camouflage my differences, or felt inferior because I wasn't able to do the things the other women were so competent at. After ten years my roughest edges had been worn away and in company I don't think I stood out quite so starkly. It was in the end, after so much heartbreak, such a simple insight, one anybody wiser or more mature than I was would have seen at once.

Now, having accepted myself for the person I was or had become, I realized I had also to accept certain conditions, one of which was that I would be lonely, that I would never be in the middle of a group of women who were intimate personal friends as I had been in the city. It was true, too much separated us, a big part of which had become my life as a professional writer, with its necessary solitude and yet its unnerving but unavoidable publicness.

But more even than my coming to an understanding of how I would live here in contentment was a growing understanding of the true nature of the long crisis which I had weathered and of the meaning of the cycle of dreams I had had. Now I saw that what I had been through was certainly triggered by the dramatic and sudden change in my life when I had left the city behind and come into an alien environment to make my life. But where for years I had thought my crisis was a particular, specific one having to do with how I would live my life in this environment, and had blamed it — this environment — for my pain, I finally began to see that it had been something else entirely.

What I had been through was a mid-life crisis, or just a major life crisis. Everyone goes through it when signs of aging can no longer be ignored and when older family members begin to die and for the first time one faces the inevitability of one's own death. But for many people it appears as vague dissatisfaction, puzzlement, depression without a clear cause, or a breaking out of the confines of one's life in destructive ways. Sometimes it results in complete breakdown. In my case, because I was largely alone, because I had a scholarly bent and an artistic nature and no very severe practical problems in my life, I allowed it to happen. I didn't fight it, but actually reveled in it, and having no one at all to help me, I resolved to understand it myself. With the help of many wonderful books, and using my journals as analyst-listener, I came through it.

Though so much of it is beyond my understanding even now, I want to say something about how nourishing, enlightening, comforting and yet disturbing Nature was to me during all of this. How my greatest insights and most disturbing experiences occurred when I was out walking alone on the prairie and how I came at last to understand my life as a part of, as a manifestation of, that larger life by which I felt myself to be surrounded. If, through Nature, I came to understand more about my own life, I also came to understand more about life. I cannot imagine how this could be done — that is, if one is a woman, and if one has no help — in the midst of a city. The only possible way to come to an understanding involving Nature is by being in Nature. And as a woman, I think coming to an understanding of and building a relationship with Nature is essential in order to understand oneself.

In my ruminations on the connection between the feminine soul I've spoken of, the Wise Woman who appeared in my dreams when I most needed her, and Nature as feminine, or women as in some respects synonymous with Nature, I can come to no hard and fast conclusions. Sometimes I think that the small vision I had the morning I began this book of that beautiful field I walk in, which I took as an omen or a blessing, was not given by the spirits of the past, as I'd thought, but was instead a manifestation of Nature itself. I wonder if the woman I saw in my dreams and that small, exquisite, soul-satisfying vision were not one and the same.

HOME

During the years that I was beating my way through the thickets of self-delusion, the world around me was not static. In fact, the agricultural world was facing a growing crisis too, a crisis of such huge proportions and breadth that everybody around me was eventually affected by it to some degree. One major factor was drought.

From my journal:

> *June 29, 1984: 11:10 a.m. It is 91 degrees F. and the wind must be blowing up to 50 m.p.h. That hot wind and lack of moisture (last July we had a 3-day rain and virtually nothing since) is ruining the hay and the grain crops. Even my vegetable and flower gardens won't grow. The sky is a pale, dusty blue at the horizon and higher up where the dust doesn't reach it, it is the usual bright blue of summer. Anxiety Butte is faded by the haze of dust in the air. The hay crop is short and thin and burning at the bottom and the crested wheat grass in the yard has whitish tips and is pale dun below. The road is crumbling to dust.*

*Everything looks white, even the air, even the grass and trees that
have been watered and are green, and the earth between the
back door and the carragana hedge is blown bare and is white
and cracking. People who are overextended are worried sick.*

1:20 p.m.: 98 degrees F.

*2:00 p.m.: 101 degrees F. in the shade of the deck. Still
blowing.*

*5:30 p.m.: A dust storm. For some time clouds — normal thun-
derclouds, not very serious-looking — had been coming from the
south and there had been thunder occasionally for about an hour.
I looked up and a dust storm was on us from the southwest.
Everything was obliterated by the fine brown air. It lasted only ten
minutes or so and then vanished and a hard rain came down
briefly. In those moments the temperature fell 20 degrees to 75
degrees F., but the wind never stopped.*

*   *   *

*July 16, 1984: All the cattle have been sent out of the P.F.R.A.
pasture three months early because all the waterholes have dried
up. The constant sound of wind in your ears.*

*   *   *

*September 1, 1984: We're almost out of water here. The river is
barely flowing.*

*   *   *

*July 29, 1985: Our grain crop has been written off 100% in all
fields.*

The summer of 1984 we set records for heat every day from July first to the eleventh. Peter reported that the hay crop was the worst since he'd taken over the hay farm in 1965 and young grasshoppers were detected everywhere in the grass. Farmers in Saskatchewan, the worst hit by the drought, began to hold the first of the drought meetings trying to get help from the government, and everybody scrambled to pull in any slack, while those in the most precarious financial position began to lose their farms. But, for the most part, people believed this was just another drought in the relatively predictable cycle of droughts, and that those who could had only to wait it out and prosperity would soon return.

I had a roof over my head and three square meals a day because Peter raised cattle for market and sold them, because he had some farmland (farmed by others), and whether it rained or not or the winds blew too hard or spring was early or late or the winter colder or warmer than usual with more or less snow were matters of importance to me as they were to the people in whose midst I was living. Hardly noticing I had, I'd begun to watch the sky for signs of rain, for cold fronts moving in, for approaching storms or blessed Chinooks, and to study cloud formations and sunsets for clues as to the next day's weather. In the early eighties when the rain began to fail, the drought was of grave interest to me for more than its sociological effects.

One major consequence was that we had to sell a liner-load of cows and calves, unheard of on the Butala ranch and which might be compared to starting to live off the capital instead of the interest from your trust fund, or like selling off parcels of your land. Peter took this step because the drought had meant there was no hay crop with which to feed them in the winter, and because no grass had grown there was no grazing either, with the result that we had to buy a lot of expensive feed. For the first time in quite a while people with cattle had an edge on those who raised only grain, because we could at least sell cattle, while people with only grain to sell, what there was of it, were encountering additional problems having nothing to do with drought.

Other factors, too, were at work which hadn't been foreseen by most farmers during the good times. Overall, farm input costs — chemical fertilizer, herbicides and pesticides, machinery and fuel — went up about three hundred percent in that ten-year period from the time the cash from the huge crops of the last half of the seventies hit the farm economy, into the early eighties when the bonanza began to dry up.

As if drought and the increase in input costs weren't bad enough, bank interest rates hit an astonishing high — up to twenty-four percent on borrowed money, and since nearly everybody ran their farms or ranches on operating loans, the fiscal system itself began to put people out of business, regardless of their continued ability to grow grain or raise livestock. By 1989 in most places the drought had ended, but it no longer mattered whether we could grow grain or not, because increasingly either we couldn't sell it or the prices we could get for it were below what it cost to produce it.

For the first time farmers had to face the fact that stiff competition in grain markets wasn't something they were going to be able to beat. Countries which had bought Canadian grain had now become exporters themselves, while others became at least self-sufficient, and as buyers became fewer, the sellers began to compete even harder and grain prices fell to lows unheard of for the generation currently on the farms. There was constant talk about the greenhouse effect — global warming — which would ruin the western climate for grain farming. And nobody was admitting it, but in parts of the Palliser Triangle the land was dying as a consequence of its being marginal farmland in the first place, of which too much had been asked for too long. It wasn't that the present was bad and growing more desperate, it was also that the future had suddenly turned from apparently limitless to a brick wall.

I was privy to the endless conversations about the situation when Peter's friends dropped in for coffee or we dropped in to their kitchens. I heard the amazement, the anger, the bitterness, the sadness, the "if" talk and the potential solutions dreamt up by this one or that one. If I was surprised at anything it was at how civilized everybody managed to be, no matter how bad his/her situation. People seemed to feel helpless to force out of the powers that be whatever changes were needed to save farms and farmers. I have the impression that most people were coming to see that no government had a clue what to do — or that governments knew what to do, but refused for political reasons to do it. There were meetings and protests, but compared to the rage of, for example, the rioters of Los Angeles who in an orgy of violence burned, looted and otherwise destroyed in response to the racism which blighted their lives, or even the vocal militance of farmers in France, the protests of prairie farmers, whose lives were also being broken in a way apparently impossible for city dwellers to imagine, seemed to me to be surprisingly muted.

But then, I think there was a part of most agricultural people which remained disbelieving, which did not fully realize the extent and apparent irreversibility of the catastrophe. Raised for a least two generations on the myth that we were "the breadbasket of the world," we didn't find it easy to look in the eye so basic a belief, the framework on which three generations had built their lives and a whole society, and see that this was no longer true and, in fact, probably never had been. If the agricultural people's fatal flaw had been hubris, and I believe it was, they had been led into it by shortsighted governments and the so-called experts who were themselves only the common people with degrees, and by agricultural corporations and financial institutions whose only mandate or interest was to make as much money as possible out of the work, the hardship, of others.

All of this has been documented in countless magazine articles, radio broadcasts and television specials, and somewhere, no doubt, somebody is writing the definitive book about the end of the family farm on the Canadian Prairies. Nothing was the way it had been ten years earlier. Wherever necessity dictated and there were jobs to be found, farm people went to work off the farm. Women who had always been available to help with farm work at home and to drive kids to after-school activities were suddenly at work in the bank, the credit union, the grocery store, school, hospital or senior citizens' lodge, jobs which might help keep body and soul together, but which had little or nothing to do with self-fulfillment, and which took women away from the satisfaction of spending the day in the midst of natural beauty. As a result of economic stress rural life was changing so quickly that the old "traditional" life was getting harder and harder to find. I had moved from the city into a world I thought was in some ways idyllic and now, with truly breathtaking rapidity, it seemed it was dying.

I began to see the lives of the people around me as not merely picturesque, interesting, or beautiful (and therefore as removed from me), but as *real*. It wasn't just that their losses were real in terms of real pain, real suffering, but that it was coming clear to me that the grain farmers of Western Canada had built the world out of their own sweat and muscle-power and bank of knowledge handed down from generation to generation — they and the members of my own family had spent their lives doing hard work with small rewards. If I found it hard to lose what I had had for such a short time — the wide, wild fields around me, the animals, the slower and more meaningful pace of life — how much harder for those who had never known any other life, nor their parents and sometimes their grandparents before them.

At the same time I was beginning to get phone calls from magazine, newspaper and radio editors and researchers who wanted someone with a proven record as a writer, who actually lived in the midst of the crisis and was directly affected by it, to write about it. This too forced me into looking at its genesis and history in a more comprehensive and fundamental way. I had to study the situation as a scholar would, with the additional advantage of having a good measure of skepticism at anything that smacked of conventional wisdom. (For the first time since I'd left the university, I found myself grateful for the training in research I'd received in grad school.) I had around me the evidence of my eyes, my own family history as westerners behind me, and the stories of the families in the Palliser Triangle, all things which most scholars and most journalists who came from Vancouver and Toronto to report on what was going on in Saskatchewan lacked.

And I had Peter, an unconventional thinker if ever there was one, clever, patient, and in whose long silences a lot of cogitation had gone on over the years. He had some clear ideas about what had gone wrong, and more, about what really mattered, what losses counted in the ongoing stream of life, and what didn't, out of which I might discern what the essence of rural life really is.

I thought of Thomas Hardy's account of the agricultural workers of late-nineteenth-century England in *Tess of the D'Urbervilles*, of Tolstoy in *Anna Karenina* writing about the Russian peasants at work on the land, of Knut Hamsun in *The Wayfarers* chronicling the lives of the working poor of Norway. I thought of Patrick White's magnificent *The Tree of Life*, and much later, of Olive Schreiner's *The Story of an African Farm*. I remembered my first attempt at writing a novel seven or eight years earlier, how it was to have been about the life of an urban, academic, single parent, how I thought I had nothing else of interest to write about. Now I saw how insular and blind I had been.

I had come to know my way around the countryside, I had stood in the midst of a field of our ruined wheat that was singing with grasshoppers, I had climbed the fence and stood with my husband in what was left after it had been destroyed by hail, I had helped pull calves in the spring, I had sat proudly in the sale ring while the auctioneer sold our big steers, and held the twitch while the vet cut out a growth on a horse's face. And I used all this, every incident, every — to me — astonishing detail of my new life, in my writing. If I could do nothing more, I told myself, I could pay intense and precise attention, I could at least make a detailed, accurate record of life here and what had happened to it that wouldn't be the self-serving version of those who had made it happen, but would be told from the point of view of the people who had lived it and suffered it.

As I write this we are calving. In the past two weeks I've been present at the births of five or six calves, running to get equipment, helping get the heifer into the barn or corral, on one occasion narrowly escaping being flattened by a cow who'd decided to leave through a gate I was standing at, not yet having made up my mind whether to go in or stay out. Peter teased me about it, saying he didn't know I could still move that fast. I never get over the excitement of seeing that calf emerge, at that moment when it opens its eyes and blinks and its sides tremble with its first breaths of air. "It's alive!" I always catch myself saying in astonishment and joy, and "Welcome to the world!" to the little creature. If the grim inevitability of death is always present in rural life, so is the never-ending surprise and joy at the birth of new life.

I don't go out every day with Peter to help him anymore. We agree that my writing is more important. I am no longer as curious as I once was, nor am I as young. He has responded to this, as most people in the business have to the lack of help, by mechanizing as far as possible. I sometimes regret this, but I know now that I would never be as content, even as happy, as some of my friends and neighbors seem to be checking pregnant heifers with a flashlight in the middle of the night, pulling calves, driving tractors, balers or combines, pickling and canning and freezing food and in the evening playing cards or making quilts or crocheting or knitting or just visiting. I envy those who find contentment in these things, because in them, it seems to me, there is a calm, a sense of peace and of the simple rightness of existence from which, for whatever reason, I have been forever barred. Nonetheless, through working with Peter all these years and sharing in the joys and the trials of this ranching life, I had been gathering another, deeper kind of understanding about rural life.

The circumstances of our neighbors and acquaintances grew more and more critical and the talk everywhere — on the streets, on coffee row, at dances and family gatherings — grew more and more despairing. Loss was everywhere around me, fear, anger and an omnipresent, inexorable sadness at the destruction of a way of life several generations old and of the dream of the future that had proven to be unattainable. In the midst of the confusion and chaos and contradictory ideas going on around me, I tried to make sense out of the desperation of farm families to stay on their farms no matter what the price. I tried to see beyond the reasons they gave when asked: because they were too old to start a new life somewhere else, or because they knew how to do nothing else, or because they knew the virtual impossibility of finding work in towns or cities in the midst of a general recession, even beyond those who called on a moral right — this was my father's and my grandfather's place and nobody is putting me off it.

Clearly there was more to this need to stay on the farm than what was being said, no matter how true these reasons were. The more I thought about it, the more I lived the life myself, the more it seemed to me that the roots of the profound sorrow and genuine desperation of farm people lay in something deeper than these things. Because I had finally come to know a life lived in Nature myself, I began to believe that, at root, the basic loss to farm people was greater even than a loss of livelihood or a familiar way of life, as hard as these things would be to endure. The greatest loss, it seemed to me, was the loss of constant contact with Nature and of all that implied.

I didn't believe the hopeful prophecies that salvation was just around the corner and that soon everything would go back to the way it had been in the late seventies. When I heard experts prophesy about even bigger and better technologies which would save us, I shuddered, since it seemed to me that it was technology run rampant that had brought on the disaster in the first place. When I heard about corporate farms I saw only a modern-day feudal system where people would work the land for the profit of landowners whose faces they would never even see. When I heard about any ideas for saving the place which involved moving people off their farms, I saw only unlivable, dangerous megalopolises full of the poor and homeless — and an empty landscape.

North America, obsessed with the notion of progress and the technological means to achieve it, and increasingly urbanized, has failed to make a place for people on the land. Thousands of people, rural for generations, have been driven off it. We have raped our natural resources and despoiled them, overused pesticides, insecticides, chemical fertilizers and huge machinery to subdue Nature, and devalued the rural person and his/her way of life along with rural culture.

It seems to me unavoidably true that the plight of the farmers is directly related to the question of our need as a species to come back to Nature. If we abandon farms and farmers as we have known them for the last ten thousand years, we abandon our best hope for redefining ourselves as children of Nature and for reclaiming our lost souls, for what other sizable body of people exists in North America with their knowledge? There are only Native people left, who have been speaking to deaf ears since their conquest from five hundred to a hundred years ago. We may at last be ready to listen to them, but the cultural differences — in particular, religion — make it difficult for many non-Natives to hear what Natives are saying. Increasingly we know in our hearts they are right, have been right all along, but we can't seem to find a way of implementing their knowledge, of blending it with our own beliefs into a workable salvation both for the land and for all of us as a species.

At the simplest level is the fact that all the values we cherish and that we consider to be the basis of our culture as a whole, and that provide for its continuity but that are difficult to keep alive in cities, live on in the country: tightly knit extended families and small communities, where the loss of any one member leaves a gap but where deviance is tolerated and doesn't mean a life on the streets, where interdependence is clear and cooperation thus a way of life, but without destroying self-reliance essential for survival in a sparsely populated countryside and in a harsh climate.

Country people understand how the world was built; it didn't appear whole and shiny the morning they were born; their fathers and mothers built it step-by-step each day. With only the most fragile and minimal of support systems rural people have learned to do everything for themselves: to build roads and houses and machinery and to grow crops to feed thousands as well as their own families. Even more precisely, each individual farmer knows his acres of land intimately, knows the weather patterns over it, knows what grows best where and why, and he knows intimately what the minute variations in the color of his crop or the way it stands mean and what he must do to rectify problems. No society can afford to wipe out the whole class of people in whom the practical knowledge laboriously passed down by generations remains alive.

Though we can't all live on the land, we have to keep a substantial proportion of us on it in order to reestablish and maintain our connection with Nature. Further, these people have to live on the land for a long time, they need a lot of time to come into tune with it, and to do so it is vital that they not be driven only by the need to feed their families and themselves, which always results in their disregarding what they know very well about the needs of the land, and to overwork it or overstock it with animals, or to plow up marginal land — that is, to exploit Nature instead of nurturing her.

It is unbelievable to me that futurists and experts at universities and in government don't see how important it is to all of us that a stable body of people remain in intimate touch with the land, and include it in their equations about the future. So far there has been no concerted effort that I know of by governments at any level to address the issue of rural depopulation in a creative way. Any efforts have so far been based on the unexamined belief that rural life and farming or ranching must be synonymous. As long as we pursue reasoning from this narrow foundation, given current market conditions and the prospect of more and more countries becoming self-sufficient or exporters of food, we are unlikely ever to find a solution that allows for a considerable, stable body of rural people.

Years ago an old man who had farmed and raised cattle on this land all his life, when we were speculating about the future for people out here given financial disaster and rapid depopulation, remarked that he thought one day there would be people on every quarter again as it had been during his childhood. I asked him how he thought this would come about. He had no answer, not conceiving of a mechanism that would produce this result, but when I asked he looked not at me but into the distance and repeated his belief. I couldn't forget what he'd said, because it seemed so clearly a visionary moment to me, beyond reason, beyond the facts. I thought he had seen something that was more than a dream, even if he had no logic with which to defend it.

Ideas for a new life out here are beginning to be heard: small, highly specific farms, medium-sized farms with a high rate of diversification, a buffalo commons with no farms at all, advanced, amazing new technology doing what we can't imagine, on enormous tracts of land, partnerships between urban families and farm families to produce food for a specific, small population, and numerous other vague and mostly unsatisfactory notions.

Much of this land, that which should never have been broken because of its marginal agricultural value, needs to be put back into grass and to do so will require money, time and a love of grasslands for themselves. Because of the extreme fragility of this landscape, any such project would require many years, probably more than one lifetime. I have no doubt that there are many people, from former farmers driven off their land to people aching to get out of the city, who would be overjoyed, if given a salary, good advice and equipment, to move onto quarter or half sections in need of reseeding and/or nurturing and to devote their lives to this project as stewards of the land.

I don't think the repopulation of the Great Plains will be easy, nor do I claim to have a clear notion of how to do it. But any such repopulation has to be based on a belief in what I have been saying, that in a renewed relationship with Nature as a people, and in a flourishing rural life, lies the salvation and the foundation of our nation. First we have to begin with the vision and with the desire; we do not lack the wit to bring it about; what we require is leadership.

Most environmentalists tend to be urban, and as Neil Evernden has shown in *The Natural Alien*, the only way they have known how to fight the corporate world and governments has been to put Nature in their terms, as manageable, sustainable resources, withholding the designation of value of another kind — its innate value — as the primary issue. This seems to me the same kind of mistake farmers made when they asked to be taken seriously by urban people by saying that farming was a business like any other business and that farm life was just like city life, except that it took place outside of cities. Those who genuinely saw it (as distinct from those who merely paid lip service to the idea) as such destroyed it. Farm life is overwhelmingly unlike city life in most ways, despite the presence of microwave ovens, dishwashers, and even the occasional swimming pool by farmhouses. True family farming has never been a business like any other business and ought never to be seen as such. What is best in farming and farm life is that it takes place, day in and day out, in the bosom of Nature.

I think of that old man's vision of a countryside dotted with houses and houses filled with families, children in small country schools, churches filled again on Sundays, weekend dances and entertainments, well-traveled roads, a vibrant, living culture flourishing far from cities. In his vision he sees this place as it was sixty or seventy years ago; I see it too, but I see a people with a different ethic than those of his childhood had.

I see them less poverty-stricken, less driven by the simple need for survival. I see them as aware of themselves as vital to the human community in providing the direct link to Nature our species must maintain. I see them as the preservers of a body of knowledge thousands of years old, as caretakers, stewards of the land, and maybe even, in a much better world than this one, as the wise men and women to whom others will turn for guidance and healing.

My mother's golden memories of life on the farm, where she had lived till she was fourteen when her father lost it to drought and my father's lifelong but hopeless dream of going back to the farm, neither of which I had paid much attention to when I was growing up, came back to me now. Now I saw that this was where I had come from; these were my people, too, whether they accepted me or not, whether I felt fully at home among them or not.

I began to feel with the immediacy of a blow to the stomach, not only what all of us would lose, but more particularly what I would lose if Peter fell victim to the crisis too. Every blade of grass, every trill from a red-winged blackbird, every sparkle of sun on the Frenchman River that trickled past our house at the hay farm seemed more precious. It seemed I had discovered a good place, a good life, just in time to lose it.

In the city for short visits now I studied people's houses, or the rows of condominiums or the new apartment buildings, assessing how close they were to each other, how big their yards were, what their occupants had for views, trying to imagine how I would live again in the city and what arrangement might be acceptable should something happen to Peter, or to the ranch. At home walking in the hills or down narrow country roads, I tried to imagine life without this space, this welcome, close presence of grass and sky. My dream of the blossoming twig took on new meaning. For without my realizing it, instead of being unable to imagine spending the rest of my life in the country, I found to my surprise that now I couldn't imagine how I might survive if I had to leave it to go back to the city to live.

THE PERFECTION OF THE
MORNING

On a wet, cold Sunday morning in late August, after I had spent a sleepless night tossing and turning, my head was buzzing with a confusing and con-fused jumble of words, ideas, memories and fragments of dreams I was too tired to put a stop to. It was a nasty morning, I was tired and out of sorts, but the dog counts on a morning run. I couldn't work, and I felt propelled to go out for other reasons which, because of my confusion and dis-ease, my altered state of consciousness, I didn't even try to isolate and clarify. In fact, I was so muddled and mentally out of control that I didn't even real-ize I was. I put on my jacket and, my dog at my side, went out.

It was as if I were being driven by some force I couldn't see or feel, but that pushed me to go quickly — I was almost running — that had taken over my brain so that I wasn't thinking rationally — I wasn't *thinking* at all — my head was simply buzzing but nothing connected to anything else and I couldn't hold on to any thought for more than the instant it took to register before it was gone again. I reached the edge of my favorite field, put one leg cleanly down a hidden badger hole to just below my knee and fell hard facedown in the grass. Not like this, came into my head. I picked myself up, half-expecting to find my leg was broken. I pulled up my pant leg; not only was it not broken, there wasn't a mark on it, and there was no pain; instead it felt hot, burning, where the flesh and bone had struck the edge of the hole the hardest. I kept on walking, going slower now, and with the frightening buzz in my brain erased. I was calmer.

Eventually I reached a small pile of rocks at a high point with a spectacular view of the countryside. It is a long, steep climb to that point, and I had not consciously chosen to go there, having had no destination in mind at any point, not even noticing where I was going. As I approached the stones, I began to feel increasingly disturbed, increasingly upset, and I had begun to go over all the possible reasons why I might feel so distressed, but there was no reason I could isolate. Yet the closer I came to the pile of stones the worse I felt. By the time I reached it the sky had closed in and it had begun to rain.

I had thought the rocks at that spot were a pile until that morning, when I realized they were actually a circle. I stepped inside the ring and knelt down and began to turn over the small stones lying loose there, to see if any of them were points. As I did this, my feeling of unease grew so strong that I actually began to cry and when I couldn't bear this anguish any longer — it kept growing and I stubbornly tried to ignore it — I jumped up, leaped out of the circle and ran a few steps down the nearby draw. But already I had begun a one-sided dialogue in my head, as if some part of me knew it was dealing with the supernatural, no matter how much the rest of me resisted, as to why I was being made to feel so terrible.

Because you are not worthy — these words popped soundlessly into my head. Angrily, still resisting with all my might whatever was happening, I asked, Why not? Because I'm not Native? Because I'm a woman? Because I haven't first purified myself by fasting and prayer? I stopped and stood to look back at the circle, and then I saw in my mind's eye a shaman in full dress — a long robe, I think, a feathered headdress — standing in the circle, facing out over the landscape, arms raised in an attitude of prayer or invocation. I knew then I had trespassed on what had been a sacred site.

It was at least a month before I dared go back there again, and when I did I took a passing folklorist with me. First, I told him about my experience; he showed not a trace of skepticism; I described the circle of stones as I remembered them: all a beautiful rosy pink granite, a perfect circle with a flat beige rock embedded in the earth in the center. We climbed to the high point and at first I couldn't find the circle! Then I went closer to what I thought was just a pile of rocks and there in the center was the flat beige rock I remembered clearly from that moment of scrabbling on my hands and knees at it, and the small stones scattered on it.

The circle was irregular, partly scattered by weather and animals, and the rocks were either not pink granite (although most of them were as nearly as I could tell), or were so covered with lichen I had to search them for bare spots to see what kind and color of rocks they were. I was shaken.

But something I had read in Jung kept tugging at my memory, and, back at the house, as sometimes happens to bookish people, when I took down Jung's autobiographical volume *Memories, Dreams, Reflections,* it opened to the section I was looking for. In it, Jung told of an experience he had in Ravenna visiting the tomb of Galla Placidia (the mother of Valentinian III, the Western Roman Emperor, for whom she ruled until he came of age, and who died in 450 A.D.), which he says was "among the most curious events in my life."

> Here, what struck me first was the mild blue light that filled the room; yet I did not wonder about this at all. I did not try to account for its source, and so the wonder of this light without any visible source did not trouble me. I was somewhat amazed because, in place of the windows I remembered having seen on my first visit, there were now four great mosaic frescoes of incredible beauty which, it seemed, I had entirely forgotten.

Jung describes the frescoes and continues:

> When I was back home, I asked an acquaintance who was going to Ravenna to obtain the pictures for me. He could not locate them, for he discovered that the mosaics I had described did not exist.

In fact, the mosaics had indeed been created in the basilica as he had known, but in the early Middle Ages they had been destroyed by fire.

I see a similarity in the two experiences, which seem to me to have to do with the falseness of our insistence on time as linear, and that what I saw in my mind's eye was perhaps a scene that took place two hundred or two thousand or more years ago on that very spot.

But further, I continued to wonder why I was unworthy to stand in that sacred circle. I wanted to think it was because I hadn't performed the ritual properly, including a three- or four-day fast first, but I seriously doubted that could be the reason since I felt forced to be there in the first place. Months passed, a year passed; I kept reading and thinking and trying to make my dreams and experiences form a coherent whole that would answer all my questions. I read much of the small amount of literature available about the beliefs of Amerindians recounted in their own words. There can be little doubt from these accounts that these societies were male dominated, that women, although having their place in them, were considered inferior to men, worse, that at least in some of the societies they were considered pure enough to take a significant part in rituals and ceremonies only during the time they were young virgins.

Not long ago I attended the funeral of a woman who was born here and who died here well into her old age. She was a rural woman, typical of her generation of rural women, who had worked hard all her life, and was skilled at all the tasks of rural women. She was an ordinary woman; she quarreled with people, she gave unstintingly to others. There was nothing remarkable about her life in any way: she never wrote a book, never had a career, never won a prize, never held a prestigious office, or had any power in the world except as the woman of her family, a power which she underused, if anything. Yet the church was packed and the crowd overflowed into the vestibule and out onto the lawn.

While the minister prayed, I tried to understand why all these people had come to her funeral, why they came to the funerals of other old women just like her, who had never made the smallest mark on the world.

Why else, I thought, but because, whether we say it out loud or not, or to ourselves or not, or to each other or not, we all know, we all understand in our hearts that women are the soul of the world.

When I was nearing the end of the first draft of this book, I dreamt that I was out walking in the hills with a herd of wild stallions. One white stallion out of the herd walked at my side, his head close to mine. I came to a basin formed by a circle of sloping green hills and lying on her side on the ground in the center of that basin was a white mare. She had just given birth to five foals. The foals were little blanketed bundles like newborns in a hospital nursery and they were suckling their mother, lying against her belly side-by-side as pups do. Several of the blankets were streaked with the mare's blood, and there was blood from the birth on the ground.

I halted at once, horrified, because I knew the stallion I'd been walking with would try to kill the foals. Already he had flown into a frenzy and the rest of the dream disintegrated in my struggle to hold his head to stop him from racing to the foals and trampling them, and in my anger at myself because I had brought the stallion there, however unwittingly, and knew I was responsible for the damage he would do if he got away from me.

When I was a young woman more than twenty-eight years ago, and had just given birth to my first and only child, I lay down one evening to rest and my psyche, my soul, transcended all the words in books, and all the art I knew of whatever kind, and all my past and even my future, to give me a vision of the oneness of the universe. For all these twenty-eight or so years since I have pondered it.

Although I felt the absolute, indisputable truth of it in every fiber of my being, saw that it was inarguable, I did not understand it, I did not know what to do with it. I absolutely could not see how my baby, my precious, fragile little son could be made of the same fabric as the grass, the trees, the sky. It was unimaginable in any sense, metaphoric or real. I had been raised in a fight against Nature for survival, educated at a university increasingly dedicated to progress, to technological transcendence, I had long been removed from any kind of true Nature, and so I rejected, could not even imagine how the vision could be true for me and for the entire human race.

A male figure walking by my side, whispering in my ear, being my intimate companion: I think it is time to let go of that figure, time to forget the books, forget conventional wisdom, let go of all that I was taught by church and school and history and by bitter experience in society. All these things tell me to discount what I have learned through these years of my life here in the landscape. They tell me that I am at worst quite crazy, a madwoman, and at the least that I am silly, self-deluded, romantic. I resist; although it is very hard, I resist with all my strength.

This morning I went out to walk along the winding dirt road that stretches by the river. It is mid-August of an unusually cold summer and already, down in this valley, the sun is rising later and to fog, which usually doesn't come till September. Although it was only 6:30 the fog had begun to dissipate. The Frenchman has carved out banks twenty, and sometimes more, feet high, below which the narrow, winding stream flows. This morning its surface was perfectly smooth, the mist, although the air was still, drifting along its surface in lazy, curling wisps. In this low, slanting light the river was the color of iron, and standing so far above it and looking down without moving, the mist appeared to me to be rising out of the water or being sucked back into it.

A muskrat appeared from under the near bank and paddled busily to the other side. Farther on a pair of ducks and their brood, hardly babies anymore, glided over the surface leaving a wake of widening satin ripples. An owl was hooting, hidden in the wolf willow on the opposite bank, its tender, feminine voice speaking some gentle message I couldn't interpret.

I thought about the perfection of the morning, tried to name what it is about the morning that is different from the rest of the day. Is it the stillness? It is true that I was out too early for gravel trucks to be rolling down the grid a mile away, and the morning was too damp for hay farmers to be out in their noisy tractors and swathers baling or cutting hay. Harvest, too, is late this year, so no combines were roaring their way across the fields above the valley. But, I thought, often on Sundays there is an all-day silence, or on rainy days or during off-seasons; whatever this perfection might be, it's more than the absence of noises made by humans and their machines.

I looked across to the hills on the far side of the valley, shrouded and muted by the fog, and at the closer hills where the mist had dissipated in the sun's rays. I thought of early afternoon during the summer when no animals are stirring, lying deep in their cool burrows or curled up in the shade of a copse of stunted poplars or saskatoons, when even the insects rest under blades of spear grass or cool red stones. Then in the intense, silent heat, hills, stones, burnouts, buffalo grass are imbued with magic, an otherworldly air descends over them.

And what about the end of the day when in the wash of golden light all blemishes fade and disappear and peace descends over the yellow grasses and the luminous sky? Then, too, there is such perfection that all desire for heaven is absorbed in the glowing, fragile plains, the radiant hills.

And in the night, the sky a swirl of glittering stars from its apex an unimaginable distance above, all the way to the precise line of the hills, in the vital darkness of its shadows, the earth has a solidity that is missing from the day, and we retreat indoors, out of the way of secrets it is not ours to know.

This morning I bent to smell a yellow clover bloom and a drop of cool, translucent dew touched and clung to the end of my nose. I stood on the bank and looked across the river at the grasses and the yellow and white blooms of cinquefoil and wild aster, at the shiny blue-gray leaves of the wolf willow lining the bank where white-taileds had made trails coming down to water every morning and evening, and where, picking choke-cherries, I'd once heard a doe talking to her fawn.

In the purity of the morning, I understand how much more there is to the world than meets the eye, I see that the world fails to dissolve at the edges into myth and dream, only because one wills it not to. Now I begin to understand the meaning of that vision. Now I see the truth of it.

SOURCES

Becker, Ernest. *The Denial of Death*. New York: The Free Press, 1973.

Bennett, John. *Northern Plainsmen: Adaptive Strategy and Agrarian Life*. Chicago: Aldine Publishing Company, 1969.

Brody, Hugh. *Maps and Dreams: Indians and the British Columbia Frontier*. Vancouver: Douglas & McIntyre, 1981.

Bullfinch, Thomas. *Bullfinch's Mythology of Greece and Rome with Eastern and Norse Legends*. New York: Macmillan Publishing Co. Inc., 1973.

Campbell, Joseph. *The Masks of God*. Vol. 1, *Primitive Mythology*. New York: Penguin Books, 1976.

Castaneda, Carlos. *Tales of Power*. New York: Simon and Schuster, 1974.

Colorado, Pamela. "Wayfinding and the New Sun: Indigenous Science in the Modern World." In *Noetic Sciences Review*. Summer 1992.

Cowie, Isaac. *The Company of Adventurers*. Toronto, William Briggs, 1913.

Dickason, Olive. *Canada's First Nations: A History of Founding Peoples from the Earliest Times*. Toronto: McClelland & Stewart Inc., 1992.

Evernden, Neil. *The Natural Alien: Humankind and Environment*. Toronto: University of Toronto Press, 1985.

Fraser, James. *The Golden Bough: The Roots of Religion and Folklore*. New York: Avenel Books, 1981.

Friesen, Gerald. *The Canadian Prairies: A History*. Toronto: University of Toronto Press, 1987. (Not cited in text)

Gimbutas, Marija. *The Language of the Goddess*. San Francisco: Harper & Row, Publishers, 1989.

Graves, Robert. *The White Goddess*. London: Faber and Faber, 1961.

Haines, John. *The Stars, the Snow, the Fire: Twenty-Five Years in the Alaska Wilderness*. New York: Washington Square Press, 1992.

Harding, Esther. *Women's Mysteries, Ancient and Modern*. London: Longman's Green & Co., 1935.

James, William. *The Varieties of Religious Experience: A Study in Human Nature*. New York: Macmillan Pubishing Co. Inc., 1961.

Jung, Carl, ed. *Man and His Symbols*. Reprint. New York: Dell Publishing Company, 1979.

Jung, Carl. *Memories, Dreams, Reflections*. New York: Random House, 1965.

Knudtson, Peter, and David Suzuki. *Wisdom of the Elders*. Toronto: Stoddart Publishing Co. Ltd., 1992.

Leopold, Aldo. *A Sand County Almanac.* The Oxford University Press, 1966.

Lopez, Barry. *Arctic Dreams: Imagination and Desire in a Northern Landscape.* New York: Bantam Books, 1987.

———. *Crossing Open Ground.* New York: Vintage Books, Random House, 1989.

Merton, Thomas. *Contemplation in a World of Action.* New York: Doubleday & Company, Inc., 1973.

———. *New Seeds of Contemplation.* New York: New Directions Publishing Corp., 1972.

Milloy, John. *The Plains Cree: Trade, Diplomacy and War, 1790 to 1870.* Winnipeg: The University of Manitoba Press, 1988.

Monroe, Robert. *Journeys Out of the Body.* New York: Doubleday & Company, 1971.

Neumann, Erich. *The Great Mother: An Analysis of the Archetype.* Princeton, N.J.: Princeton University Press, 1963.

———. "Mystical Man." In *The Mystic Vision,* edited by Joseph Campbell. Princeton, N.J.: Princeton University Press, 1990.

Redgrove, Peter. *The Black Goddess and the Sixth Sense.* London: Paladin, Grafton Books, 1989.

Rich, Adrienne. *Of Woman Born: Motherhood as Experience and Institution.* New York: Virago Press, 1986.

Richards, J., and K. Fung, *Atlas of Saskatchewan.* Saskatoon: University of Saskatchewan, 1969.

Saville, Ann, ed. *Between and Beyond the Benches: Ravenscrag.* Ravenscrag: Ravenscrag History Book Committee, 1982.

Shuttle, Penelope, and Peter Redgrove. *The Wise Wound: Menstruation and Everywoman.* London: Paladin, Grafton Books, Revised edition, 1986.

Spry, Irene, ed. *The Papers of the Palliser Expedition, 1857–1860.* Toronto: The Champlain Society, 1968.

Tobias, John. "Canada's Subjugation of the Plains Cree, 1879–1885." In *Sweet Promises: A Reader on Indian–White Relations in Canada,* edited by J.R. Miller. Toronto: University of Toronto Press, 1991.

Underhill, Evelyn. *Mysticism: A Study in the Nature and Development of Man's Spiritual Consciousness.* New York: The New American Library, Inc., 1974.

van der Post, Laurens. *The Lost World of the Kalahari.* London: Penguin Books, 1962.

Woodman, Marion. *Addiction to Perfection: The Still Unravished Bride.* Toronto: Inner City Books, 1982.

———. *The Pregnant Virgin: A Process of Psychological Transformation.* Toronto: Inner City Books, 1985.

A NOTE FROM THE AUTHOR

I owe thanks to many people for their influence on my life, and hence, their contribution to this book, but for practical reasons, I've tried to narrow my gratitude down to a few specific individuals and groups. I owe thanks to the women of the Divide-Claydon area and to those from the valley near Eastend who befriended me and taught me much. The writers who came to stay in the Wallace Stegner House in Eastend during the time I was working on this book also provided support and encouragement, in particular, Sean Virgo and Terry Jordan. Nor would this book be as extensive, as detailed, or as comprehensible as it is without the sensitivity and incisiveness of my editor, Phyllis Bruce, who often seemed to know what I was trying to say when I wasn't sure myself. Any shortcomings in the book are my responsibility. Thanks to all of them, and especially to Peter and my family, without whose loving support I would have given up long ago.